Let's Save
ANTARCTICA!

James N. Barnes
Photography by Eliot Porter

Greenhouse Publications

First published in 1982 by
Greenhouse Publications Pty Ltd
385-387 Bridge Road,
Richmond 3121
Victoria, Australia

Copyright © James N. Barnes, 1982

Designed by Andrena Millen
Typeset by Meredith Typesetters
Printed and bound by Dai Nippon,
Tokyo

ISBN 0 909104 45 X

Cover photograph:
Killer whale and Adelie penguins,
McMurdo Sound, Antarctica

Acknowledgements

I owe a large debt of gratitude to two friends who really are responsible for this book. Carolina Karasik, the poet, first encouraged me to write it, and gave me many invaluable suggestions. Suzanne Arnold worked tirelessly and creatively with me to put the book in a readable form and introduced me to the publisher: without her loving efforts the book would never have been completed.

Special appreciation also must go to Eliot Porter, who so generously contributed his beautiful photographs of the Antarctic.

I am enormously grateful to a number of other friends who unstintingly gave their time to review drafts and encouraged the effort. They include Barbara Mitchell, Michael M'Gonigle, Robert Hofman, Sidney Holt, James Deane, Francoise Burhenne, Robert Boote, Michael Kennedy, Ilona Roberts, Sir Peter Scott.

The Center for Law and Social Policy allowed me the freedom to work on Antarctic issues from 1977-80. Without the support of my colleagues there, including Leonard Meeker, Clif Curtis, and Judith Roberts, I would never have been in a position to write the book.

Fund for Animals staff in Australia gave generously of their time to help produce the drafts, especially Barbara and Karla, as did the staff of the International Fund for Animal Welfare in Australia.

A special note of thanks is due to Russell Train, President of World Wildlife Fund, United States, who made grants to the Center to support my Antarctic work, and to Vincent Serventy of World Wildlife Fund, Australia, who helped with finances for the book and the Antarctic and Southern Ocean Coalition.

To my daughters Deborah and Sociana

Foreword

Although so far away, and in spite of its inhospitable climate, more and more people are coming to recognize the importance of Antarctica. I have been fortunate enough to go there five times and found it an awe-inspiring continent of amazing beauty and interest. So far, the mountains and glaciers, the colonies of penguins and seals, and the krill in the sea which is the foundation species for all the other fauna, have escaped over-exploitation by man. The great whales alone were brought close to extinction by the whaling nations, and they are now at last being given a chance to recover.

But the threats to the wildlife and to the whole environment from the exploitation of krill, fish, oil and other minerals are now building up very rapidly, as this book recounts. If this is allowed to develop unchecked, it seems likely that we shall once again find ourselves killing the geese that lay the golden eggs. For example, until we know very much more about the populations of krill, we must not allow the huge catches which are now being suggested. And until we can be absolutely sure of preventing the irretrievable harm that could be caused by oil spills in the Antarctic environment, we must not allow the oil that is probably there to be exploited.

These are the reasons why I find the idea of making Antarctica an international park so exciting. The continent could then be protected in the same way as national parks are protected all over the world. People may think the Antarctic is remote, but there is fast-growing realization that the conservation of its rich wildlife, scenery and natural resources is of vital long-term importance to us all.

We, who share the earth with all other living things, must not squander the heritage of future generations of life on earth.

Sir Peter Scott

Photographer's Perspective

The Antarctic. A harsh desert land of ice-encased mountains, of the flightless penguin and hardy pelagic birds, of seals and whales.

And for all its grim and hostile character, Antarctica with its pristine snows, its unbelievable clarity of air, and its blue, cascading ice, is sublimely beautiful. The atmosphere is so clear that one is easily deceived by distances; mountains that seem no more than 100 kilometres away may be 400. And in the absence of haze, the colours of distant objects are not like those in other parts of the world.

Antarctica is a region where man's presence has been minimal, where he never ventured and could not survive before he was able to bring with him, by means of his technology, enclaves of the temperate climate of his origin.

Antarctica has escaped the fate of other continents until modern technology made its penetration possible.

Already the damage is enormous, Adelie penguins are declining as a result of human disturbance. Fur seals were nearly wiped out by the depredations of sealers. Whales in great numbers and many kinds once roamed the sub-Antarctic seas; today, because of the efficiency, persistence, and greed of the Japanese, Russian, and Norwegian whaling fleets, they are rarely seen.
whaling fleets, they are rarely seen.

The blue whale, the largest animal ever to have lived on earth, has been brought near to extermination.

The exploitation of krill has already begun. By the time the Antarctic Treaty is susceptible to change in 1991, the pressures to exploit the continent's resources of food, fuel and minerals may well be irresistible.

Drilling on the land alone for oil and minerals will surely and irreversibly change the character of Antarctica. The great, wild beauty of Antarctica will be corrupted by trash and pollution.

Oil spills from tankers or wells would have an incalculably damaging effect on the marine life. Seals could not escape the adverse indirect effect; oil-soaked penguins would die by the thousands and their rookeries would be eventually decimated.

The predictable consequences of economic exploitation of the last untouched land on the planet demand critical and well researched decisions.

This handbook will allow concerned people to make the choice for themselves. It will allow them to influence Governments.

Eliot Porter

Contents

Contents

Photographs on next 8 pages
  1. Weddell seal, Humble Island, Antarctica Peninsula, February 1976
  2. View down Beacon Valley, Antarctica, December 1975
  3. Emperor penguins, McMurdo Sound, December 1975
  4. The giant Blue whale, now so rare, in Antarctic waters
  5. Crabeater seals, Deception Island, Antarctic Peninsula, February 1976
  6. Bull Fur seal, Litchfield Island, Antarctic Peninsula, February 1976
  7. Gentoo penguins, Deception Island, Antarctic Peninsula, February 1976
  8. Green iceberg, Livingston Island, Antarctic Peninsula, March 1976

Introduction

This is a handbook to help concerned people save Antarctica. The aims of the handbook are:

- to present an overview of facts and environmental issues concerning the area;
- to enable people everywhere to help protect this unique, rich region from environmental devastation;
- to give practical information about the present political situation, treaty status and countries involved;
- to educate and inform the general public and decision makers on these issues;
- to alert people to the consequences of environmental devastation of Antarctica.

People *can* play an effective role in influencing political decision made by governments. The protection of this region's ecosystems and marine life must concern governments, everywhere.

Antarctica is the common heritage of all humans; by the end of this century it will be seen as the last great sanctuary where large wild populations of mammals and birds can live, feed and breed in their natural environment. It should be protected, understood and treasured for generations to come.

Antarctica must become a World Park or Global Preserve — protected from mineral exploitation forever. You can help make the World Park a reality.

Why is Antarctica Under Threat?

The energy hungry nations seek oil and minerals with increasing urgency. The Antarctic region is thought to contain large amounts of oil and gas. Oil companies and governments want to explore and exploit the region. The Antarctic Treaty nations have begun secret negotiations on a new treaty which would allow this to happen.

Many nations are keen to reap the harvest of Antarctica's ecosystems. Krill, the foundation species for all of Antarctica's wildlife, is their primary target. There are proposals pending for harvesting penguins, and some companies seem interested in killing seals again.

If these interests are allowed to exploit the region, the results may be irreversible. Antarctic ecosystems could be destroyed. Some of the *species* threatened by commercial exploitation are listed here.

- Great Whales, *already near extinction, will be severely threatened because of over-harvesting of krill.*
- Seals — *millions of seals — Crabeater, Weddell, Leopard, Ross, Southern Elephant and Fur Seals would be jeopardized.*

- Birds — *millions of penguins, albatrosses, fulmars, petrels, cormorants, skuas, terns and gulls live in the Antarctic for all or part of the year.*
- Lichens *and Antarctic vegetation will disappear. Very little is known about this unique growth.*
- Fish — *overfishing in the area has already jeopardized some species. If this overfishing continues, many more will be in a critical state.*

What are some other Reasons why Antarctica should be Protected?

Antarctica serves several important and unique functions.
- It is our best monitoring zone for measuring global pollution
- It now is an international, scientific preserve containing secrets of the Earth's past.
- The Antarctic ice cap is a key to our global climate. Any change to the ice cap could have devasting results.

Exploitation of minerals will cause major controversy between richer and less developed countries because the former group retains control of the region's resources and all decision making with regard to their exploitation. Only token benefits from any exploitation will go to the less-developed countries.

What are Conservationists and Environmentalists trying to Accomplish?

Environmental and conservation organizations have several main goals concerning Antarctica and the Southern Ocean.
1. The Antarctic region should be completely protected from all mineral and oil exploration and exploitation, and given status of a World Park, Global Preserve or International Heritage Monument.
2. The World's first 'Ecosystem' fishing regime, the Convention on the Conservation of Antarctic Marine Living Resources, must be properly implemented and enforced. This means that all fishing for krill and other marine life should take place only as part of a scientific experiment.
3. No actions should be taken by nations, companies or individuals which further jeopardize endangered and threatened species in the region, particularly whales.
4. The region should continue to be demilitarized and no nuclear activities should be allowed.
5. Resumption of commercial sealing should not be allowed, and nor should exploitation of penguins be permitted.

How can I Help?

You can support the Antarctic and Southern Ocean Coalition (ASOC), which now has members in twenty-two countries. You can join the Antarctica Project, a new international citizens' organization, devoted to protecting Antarctica.

Contribution and membership forms are included in this book. More information about ASOC and The Antarctica Project can be obtained from:

Michael Kennedy, PO Box 371, Manly NSW 2095, Australia
Jim Barnes, 1751 N. St. NW, Washington, DC 20036, USA

You can write to your government and the United Nations urging tha Antarctica be preserved as a World Park or Preserve.

You can circulate petitions to your fellow citizens which call on the Antarctic Treaty governments to fully protect the region. A copy of the World Park petition is included in this book.

We will give more detailed information about how you can help later.

The basic legal arrangement for decision making in the area is known as the Antarctic Treaty. This treaty comes up for review in 1991. It was signed by twelve nations in 1959 and currently has fourteen full voting members or Consultative Parties. They are: Argentina, Australia, Belgium, Chile, Federal Republic of Germany, France, Japan, New Zealand, Norway, Poland, South Africa, USSR, United Kingdom and the United States of America.

The Antarctic Treaty does not answer the question — 'Who owns resources in the region?'

The Consultative Parties to the Antarctic Treaty have negotiated new legal treaties to cover harvesting of seals and all marine life in the region. These treaties must be properly implemented.

A new treaty to cover exploitation and regulation of mineral resources is being actively pursued by the fourteen Consultative Parties. Their governments will conduct a series of special secret negotiations during the next few years to develop a minerals treaty, and obviously this would allow mineral development.

The fourteen members of the Antarctic Treaty 'Club' have been doing their best to keep Antarctic policy decisions low key and closely held. Much basic information about Antarctic decision-making is shrouded in secrecy, and no environmental, conservation or scientific organizations are permitted to attend Antarctic Treaty Meetings.

The international political situation with regard to the area is complex, with the Treaty Parties themselves sharply divided on the question of national claims to sovereignty: seven Treaty nations claim sections of Antarctica, while the other Treaty members dispute those claims. Some of the claims overlap each other. The claims are shown on the map on page 17.

Other countries of the world have been largely silent on the issues. But many less developed nations believe Antarctica should be included, with the deep oceans, as part of the 'Common Heritage of Mankind'.

Our ignorance of Antarctica must be kept in mind. Our knowledge about the region's marine ecosystems is very limited. Our ability to predict accurately the possible impacts of commercial resource exploitation is also extremely limited.

A central theme of all efforts to protect the region must be the need for greatly increased research, covering all aspects of the region's ecological structure.

The history of Antarctica has been spoiled by the wanton slaughter of whales, penguins and seals during the last 100 years. Today, this killing has largely been stopped. The wild and untouched landscape and seas of the region are a continuing reminder of nature's majesty. It is the world's largest wildlife sanctuary.

Antarctica is unique and should be treated as a special place. We must protect Antarctica.

Political Background on Antarctica

11

Why Do We Care About Antarctica?

The Continent   The Antarctic can be broken down into four components: the continent proper, the Antarctic peninsula and oceanic islands, the continental shelf[1], and the oceans around the continent. Antarctica is the only land mass that can be regarded as part of the Global Commons.

The continent is fairly pristine. The scenery is spectacular. There are beautiful mountains, canyons rivalling the Grand Canyon, fragile fresh water ponds and ancient lichens.

Only around scientific stations have human activities caused problems so far. Around the bases, the major problem is waste disposal. A nuclear power reactor maintained by the United States at McMurdo leaked low grade material requiring many tons of contaminated earth to be removed. It has since been dismantled. The old, dismantled whaling stations adversely affected local areas, but left no lasting damage to any region.

Less than 2 per cent of the continent is ice free, even during the southern summer. Only a small portion of those areas are along the coast, and they are the home and breeding ground for millions of birds, penguins and seals. It is these areas that would be most attractive for commercial oil and mineral facilities, just as they already are for scientific stations.

Antarctica, and its immense ice cap, plays an important role in relation to global environment, climate and weather. The role is still not understood, although many research projects are giving us important facts.

The continent is surrounded by a belt of pack ice which ranges from approximately 1.5 million square miles (4 million km²), to 8 million square miles (22 million km²), depending on the season. This pack ice is predominantly first year replacement ice, and moves in response to the winds, perhaps as much as 65 kilometres a day.

The Antarctic ice pack has an important, although poorly understood, influence on regional and global climate patterns. Because of thermal insulating properties, it greatly reduces the exchange of heat between the atmosphere and the ocean. Its large annual fluctuation in size also affects world climate.

---

[1]The continent has an area of approximately 54 million square miles (140 million kms). The continental shelf is relatively narrow and deep, with a mean width of 18 miles (30 km) and up to 860 yards (800 metres) deep. Much of the shelf is covered by ice shelves and grounded ice. It has an area of about 1.5 million square miles (4 million km²) and the ice shelves cover another 0.6 million square miles (1.5 million km²).

The ice shelves cover about half the coastline, and periodically drop off tabular icebergs up to 96 × 43 miles (160 = 72 km) in area and up to 1500 feet (450 metres) thick.

The ice pack plays a very important part in the biological productivity of the Southern Ocean and is a critical habitat for many species.

Local pollution could produce changes in the sea ice which could have a significant effect on both large-scale atmospheric circulation and local biological productivity.

Antarctica contains about 90 per cent of the world's fresh water (locked in the ice cap). Any human activity that markedly changed the thermal properties of the ice cap would be a matter of real significance. For example if the reflectance of sun from the ice was *lowered* because of an oil spill or dust from mining activities, it could have a huge impact on global climate and weather. It is thought that a large spill in pack ice would affect the heat balance, thus altering the sea/ice ratio. This could consequently affect global sea levels, threatening coastal cities everywhere.

Precipitation on the surface of the ice sheet adds to the sheet slowly. Despite the tremendous volume of potential water stored as ice, Antarctica must be considered as one of the world's greatest deserts. The average precipitation (water equivalent) is only about 2 inches per year over the polar plateau.

Melting and calving of icebergs from glaciers and iceshelves depletes the sheet. Commercial utilization of icebergs has been considered by several countries. Little attention has been given to the possible environmental effects of the artificial diversion of icebergs. These include danger to other shipping, modification of climate, and ecological changes.

The continent contains both salt and fresh water lakes, many virtually unique in the life they support. These lakes are very fragile.

There are many minerals besides oil in Antarctica, including copper, molybdenum, chromium, platinum, lead, zinc, silver, tin, gold, coal and iron. But oil is the commodity presently of most interest to companies and governments. Some experts have suggested a high-grade find of plantinum could be of commercial interest, in the near future.

Any mining or oil operations would have substantial adverse impacts on the continent and surrounding oceans, both directly and as a result of increased shipping operations. Oil development activities, for example, would require construction of substantial structures and facilities along the coast.

One way to put this in perspective is to examine the impacts of existing stations and the small tourist industry. Although both are curtailed substantially by cost and regulations of the Antarctic Treaty, conflicts with Antarctic wildlife are increasing.

The twenty-nine coastal research stations compete directly with wildlife for the ice-free areas. Little thought is given to such conflicts when new stations are opened or older ones expanded. Coastal waters will be used for dumping rubbish. Underwater photography at the bottom of McMurdo Sound reveals old vehicles, fuel drums, beer cans and clothing. Ships routinely pump their bilges offshore, and oil slicks are becoming common. Human waste at many research stations goes directly into the ocean.

The fundamental character of the continent would be jeopardized by oil or other mineral development and exploitation.

Southern Ocean

The Southern Ocean is the body of water surrounding the Antarctic continent. This huge marine ecosystem is unique, as one krill species, *Euphausia superba*, directly or indirectly helps to support all the higher species including whales, seals, penguins, seabirds, fish and squid.

The Southern Ocean extends out to the Antarctic Convergence[2]. Biological communities differ on each side of the Convergence. In particular, true Antarctic krill, the foundation species of the entire Southern Ocean ecosystem, live only south of the Convergence.

A group of fifteen governments concluded the Convention on the Conservation of Antarctic Marine Living Resources in May 1980 and agreed to establish the boundaries of the new Convention by a series of co-ordinates that approximate the Convergence. That boundary is required to develop an 'ecosystem' approach to the protection and use of marine life in the Antarctic.

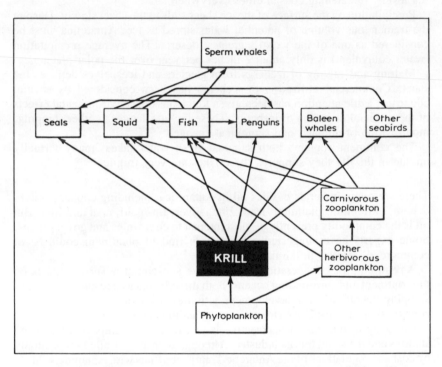

Krill form the central link in the Antarctic food web — both at sea and (via the seabirds and the nutrients their droppings bring to the nesting sites) on the land.

[2]The Convergence is a physical transition zone lying between 47°S and 63°S. Here warmer and more saline waters moving south meet the colder, fresher water coming from iceberg melt.

Antarctica is surrounded by three continuous basins of the Pacific, Atlantic and Indian Oceans. Three major types of water masses surround the continent: Antarctic surface water, which incorporates fresh water from melting ice and snow, flows northerly until it reaches the Convergence; the warm deep layer, which is very salty and low in oxygen, originates in major oceans to the north; and Antarctic bottom water which is very salty and has high oxygen content. All of these water masses play important roles in nutrient flows both within and outside the region.

The Southern Ocean has short food chains channelling energy into higher levels of the food web with great efficiency.

In its relatively pristine state, the ecosystem supports an almost unbelievable abundance of birds, seals, whales and other species. At present scientists know relatively little about species of the region, their complex interactions with each other and their physical environment.

Although huge numbers of whales have been killed in the Southern Ocean in the last century, we know little about the response of other species to the 'extra' krill supposedly made available by the large reduction of whales. Recent research suggests that crabeater seals and minke whales have increased greatly, probably by eating that krill.

The Southern Ocean is relatively deep, generally 4000 to 5000 metres, with only limited areas of shallow water. It has a complex system of currents and upwelling of nutrient-rich water. The abundant nutrients contribute to high rates of phytoplankton growth (on which krill feeds) in the Southern summer.

Because it is far removed from commercial development, the Southern Ocean serves as a unique reference point for evaluating climatic changes and global pollution levels. It can tell us how we are poisoning our planet.

Krill

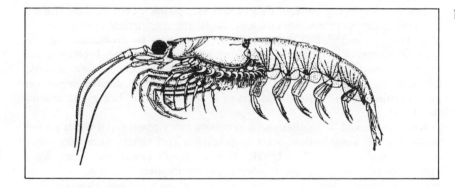

Krill, Euphausia superba, *is a shrimp-like crustacean, 3 inches (7.5 centimetres) long overall.*

The icy waters around Antarctica are the home of enormous populations of krill, shrimplike crustaceans of high protein value which are dependent on phytoplankton and form the basis of the entire Antarctic marine ecosystem.

The principal krill species, *Euphausia superba*, attains a relatively large size (5 to 6 centimetres, 2 to 3 inches), forms dense swarms (sometimes several hundred metres across and 15 to 20 metres deep[3]), and is widely distributed around the Antarctic continent.

[3]Recently the largest school of krill ever tracked was found near Elephant Island. It took up several square kilometres of sea, went to 600 feet (200 metres) in depth, and was estimated to contain about 10,000 metric tons (1/7 of last year's total world marine catch of all fish species).

Some scientists and fishing experts believe krill could be one of the world's largest untapped food resources. Only a few years ago scientists in the USSR estimated the annual yield of krill could be 70 million metric tons per year, or the equivalent of the present harvest from *all* the rest of the world's oceans.

Many scientists now feel safe harvests must be dramatically lower — 2 million tonnes or less — to avoid adversely affecting other species. Even harvests of less than 2 million tonnes could jeopardize recovery of the endangered baleen whales — blue, fin and humpback — because of direct competition for the same large swarms of krill.

Commercial interest in krill began about fifteen years ago, largely as a result of Russian and Japanese surveys. In recent years about a dozen nations have carried out research and/or experimental fishing for krill. Technology has been developed for catching, processing and preparing krill for commercial use.

It is difficult to predict how quickly the new Antarctic krill fishery will develop, but a possibility of rapid build-up exists. During 1979 the total krill harvest was probably less than 200,000 tonnes. Some believe the harvest doubled in the 1980-81 season. The USSR is reported to have taken one million tons of krill and fin fish in the region during the 1981-82 season. Until the new Marine Living Resources Convention is operating, no precise statistics will be available.

Nations developing the krill fishery still face obstacles before their fishing and processing operations are efficient. So far the commercial products available have not established large markets. There may be problems with the fluoride content of krill, restricting its consumption by humans. Technological problems, however, are expected to be overcome in the next two or three years, while consumer demand will depend to some considerable degree on price considerations.[4] Already dozens of krill products are being sold around the world.

Krill meal could be an alternative to certain other commercial meals on the world market. Some nations want to develop a krill fishery to replace other distant water fisheries. The USSR, Poland, South Korea and Japan were closed out of many areas when other countries imposed 200 mile (333 kilometre) exclusive fishery zones in recent years. Many traditional fisheries have collapsed from overfishing. The distant water fishing fleets turn inexorably to new areas. No other area is so interesting to these fleets as the Antarctic.

Until recently marine life in the Southern Ocean other than whales and seals was not subject to any form of management. Under the new Convention on the Conservation of Antarctic Marine Living Resources, all nations will be required to observe the regulations applying the 'ecosystem' approach.

Theoretically this should lead to the conservation of all species, whether or not directly harvested. *An important goal for environmental and conservation organizations is to ensure that the ecosystem standard contained in the new Convention is properly implemented*. This will be difficult, because the voting rules of the Convention do not favour conservation, and even if one member nation objects to a rule, it cannot be enacted.

Years of sophisticated research are needed before safe harvest levels of krill can be set. But the nations involved are not yet willing to pay for this research.

[4]The International Institute for Environment and Development has studied the potential krill fishery extensively. Their report, *The Management of the Southern Ocean*, by Barbara Mitchell and Richard Sandbrook, is an excellent source of information.

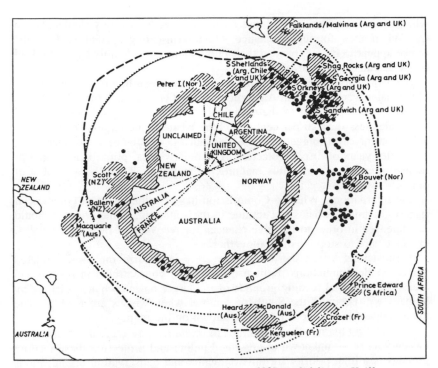

*The Antarctic Treaty area extends to 60°S (solid line). Krill are
found south of the Antarctic Convergence (dashed line). The
Convention deals with the fishery within the convergence, which has
been precisely defined (dotted line). The main known concentrations
of krill are shown as dots; some of the big densities seem to be
within the areas disputed by Argentina and the United Kingdom.*

We do not know if there is more than one population of krill in the Southern
Ocean. Details about the life cycle, reproduction and feeding behaviour are
incompletely known. We do not even know why krill swarm.

Excess harvesting could deplete krill or change krill swarming behaviour.
It could lead to replacement of krill as the dominant herbivore in the ecosystem.
The replacement species might be less acceptable or available to predators,
permanently altering the basic structure of Southern Ocean ecosystems.

Whales

In spite of the fact that whaling has been under international regulation for
decades,[5] most whale populations in Antarctica have continued to fall.[6] Larger

[5]Southern right whales were protected in 1931, blue and humpback whales in 1963,
fin and sei whales in 1978.

[6]The whales in the region fall into two major categories, baleen and toothed. Baleen
whales occurring in Antarctica include blue, pigmy blue, fin, sei, minke, humpback
and southern right. Toothed whales occurring in Antarctica include sperm, killer,
hourglass dolphin, dusky dolphin, Peal's dolphin, Commerson's dolphin, Southern
right-whale dolphin, long-finned pilot whale, spectacled porpoise, southern bottle-
nose whale and Arnoux's beaked whale.

17

whales (blue, humpback, fin and right) have been severely depleted to a fraction of their former abundance. Other krill-eating species such as the minke appear to have expanded their populations considerably by taking krill formerly eaten by larger whales.

In a 1981 survey by IWC scientists, only seventeen humpbacks and seven blue whales were spotted in Antarctic waters. It is estimated that blue whales are less than 5 per cent of their original stock, humpbacks 3 per cent, and fin whales less than 20 per cent. The blue whale is the largest creature ever to live on the earth, bigger than the dinosaur. Its population is not increasing even after years of direct protection. The blue whales' plight is a symbol of human greed. If we save this magnificent mammal, it will be a symbol of our new awareness.

The International Whaling Commission has permitted a small commercial fishery for minke whales to continue in the Antarctic. Some argue it should be increased in order to improve chances for recovery of the larger whales. Others desire to stop whaling altogether.

A substantial krill fishery could severely jeopardize the more depleted baleen whale populations. Krill fishing will be concentrated in open-ocean areas, the principal feeding grounds of the larger baleen whales. Fishing by humans will occur in the Southern summer when whales are feeding. The main areas of krill concentration are shown on the map.

A critical problem is the location of the *main feeding grounds* of the larger baleen whales — unknown at present. Finding and protecting these feeding grounds is a high priority for environmental and conservation organizations around the world.

Oil exploration and exploitation activities could adversely affect whales in a wide variety of ways: interference with feeding, migration, breathing and communication. A large spill could be devastating to the whales.

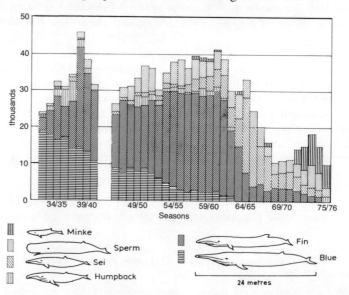

Catches in Antarctica from 1922/3 to 1975/6; the war years 1940/1 to 1945/6, when whaling was greatly reduced, are omitted. Whaling has successively reduced the Blue, Fin, Humpback and Sei whales until they became too rare to catch.

There are Crabeater, Weddell, Leopard, Ross and Southern elephant seals on the mainland and peninsula, while three varieties of Southern fur seals are found on the sub-Antarctic islands. Crabeaters alone account for close to half the world's population of seals. Its name is a misnomer: the crabeater seal eats mainly krill. No current commercial harvest takes place and all seal stocks appear to be healthy and thriving[7], although last century the fur and elephant seals were almost exterminated.

Fur seals have been increasing around South Georgia and the South Shetlands since the early 1970s. Scientists believe population increases were due to increased availability of krill, as a result of reduction in whale stocks.

Large krill fishing fleets have conducted experimental fishing in the Bransfield Strait in front of Clarence and Elephant Islands. Some observers have noted decreases in fur seal stocks during the last few years in areas where there has been significant krill fishing, including South Georgia, Clarence Island and Elephant Island. This indicates that seals could be adversely affected by a commercial krill fishery, and perhaps by finfishing as well. There is insufficient data on which to base predictions of safe harvests of krill and finfish from the standpoint of effects on seals.

In the last twenty years the USSR, Norway and Japan have seriously considered the possibility of harvesting crabeater seals. The USSR took about 1000 experimentally in 1971-72. In 1964 a Norwegian venture killed over 1100 crabeaters. Weddell seals are killed for dog food at some Antarctic research stations.

The primary risk to Antarctic seals is from habitat destruction caused by oil exploration and exploitation activities. Seals are sensitive to disturbance of their breeding grounds by humans. Beaches where elephant and fur seals live would be disturbed. The fast ice and pack ice on which Weddell, Crabeater, Leopard and Ross seals are dependent could be contaminated by industrial activities.

Seals

Fish have been exploited commercially in the Southern Ocean since the mid-1960s. Total catch cannot be determined reliably because statistical areas established by the United Nations Food and Agriculture Organization did not until recently correspond with the limits of the Southern Ocean. Not all countries report their catches accurately, if at all.[8]

Fish and Squid

[7]Populations are estimated as follows: Crabeater (30,000,000), Weddell (1,000,000), Leopard (200,000), Ross (200,000), Southern elephant (600,000) and fur (500,000). Ross, elephant and fur seals are fully protected by the 1972 Sealing Convention while others are subject to quotas and conventional management principles.

An annual harvest of 175,000 crabeater, 12,000 leopard and 5,000 Weddell seals is permitted. The Convention also establishes a closed season from March 1 to August 31, provides six sealing zones (each of which is closed to sealing from year to year in rotation), and three reserves in which it is forbidden to kill or capture seals.

[8]Only limited information on biomass and production is available for Antarctic fish, not generally organized in a useful way. There is little detailed analysis of information suitable for fishery management decisions. The recent BIOMASS Report Series No. 12 (1980) expresses concern about the *potential* for overfishing of the following populations:
1. Scotia Sea (includes South Georgia): *Notothenia rossi marmorata, Notothenia gibberifrons, Dissostichus eleginoides, Champsocephalus gunnari, Chaenocephalus aceratus, Pseudochaenichthys georgianicus, Micromesistius australia;*
2. Kerguelen: *Notothenia rossi rossi, Dissostichus eleginoides.*

Only about 100 species of fish have been recorded in the seas south of the Convergence so far, another indication of the specialized environment involved. The Southern Ocean does not contain dense shoals of pelagic fish. Coastal zones are dominated by Nototheniids (mainly Antarctic cod and ice-fish). Many species are small, over half not attaining a length of 10 inches (25 centimetres).

Growth rates are low. Although limited information is available on reproductive cycles, sexual maturity does not seem to occur in many of the commercially exploited species until the fish are several years old. It would seem Antarctic finfish are vulnerable to overfishing. The most heavily fished zones are around South Georgia and Kerguelen Islands, and the most commercially attractive species appear to be Blue Whiting, Patagonian Hake in the south Atlantic, Antarctic cod and ice-fish in all areas.

Statistics available indicate rapid build-ups of catch by the USSR in one or two years with a commensurate drop-off, indicating overfishing for certain species.

The large number of sea-birds, elephant seals and toothed whales in the Southern Ocean, that feed partly or wholly on squid, indicates that there are large populations of cephalopods. Very little is known about them, except that they are a primary food for sperm whales. Clearly squid have an important role in the Antarctic Marine ecosystem.

Birds   The Antartctic region is an important habitat for an astounding number of birds. It is estimated that over 100 million breed there each year.

Whether migrating to Antarctica to feed, or spending their lives there, birds find conditions enabling them to thrive. In the Southern summer air, land and ice are thick with millions of birds.

There are seven major families of birds that spend all or part the year in Antarctica: Penguins[9], Albatrosses[10], Fulmars and Petrels[11], Cormorants[12], Skuas[13], Terns[14], Gulls.[15] The stately Emperor penguin breeds on the continent in the darkness of winter. The male incubates the single egg, waiting for spring.

[9]Emperor, king, adelie, chinstrap, gentoo, macaroni. The adelies are by far the most numerous, with many rookeries, estimated at over 250,000 birds. Roger Tory Peterson's book, *Penguins*, contains wonderful photographs and drawings of Antarctic penguins.
[10]Wandering, black-browed, grey headed. The albatross is the most magnificent sea-bird. It breeds only on subantarctic islands.
[11]Southern giant fulmar, southern fulmar, Antarctic petrel, cape pigeon, snow petrel, narrow-billed prion, Antarctic prion, fulmar prion, blue petrel, great-winged petrel, white-headed petrel, kerguelen petrel, soft-plumaged petrel, mottled petrel, white-chinned petrel, sooty shearwater, Wilson's storm petrel, South Georgia petrel and Kerguelen diving petrel. Nine nesting areas are known for the Antarctic Petrel, which spends all of its life in the region.
[12]Blue-eyed shag.
[13]South polar skua, brown skua.
[14]Antarctic tern, arctic tern. The arctic tern flies 18,000 miles (29,000 kilometres) each year to feed in the Antarctic during the summer.
[15]Southern black-backed gull.

There are large gaps in our knowledge of Antarctic birds, regarding abundance, distribution, population dynamics and feeding patterns.

The most serious threats to Antarctic birds will come from pollution, destruction of habitat, and reduction of food supplies. Development of large fisheries for krill or finfish would put pressure on birds. But there have been recent proposals for harvesting penguins. A Japanese company has been negotiating with Argentina to kill 48,000 magellan penguins yearly as a pilot project, reportedly for gloves. This could be the precursor to reviving a commercial penguin industry in the Antarctic. From 1895 to 1919 over 150,000 king penguins were killed each year on MacQuarie Island — for their tiny quantities of oil.

Terrestrial Vegetation

On the continent there are only two flowering plants. More than 400 species of lichens, including some unique to Antarctica, and about 200 species of bryophytes have been identified.

The taxonomic status of Antarctic vegetation is poorly known. Most vegetation occurs in the maritime Antarctic and coastal areas of the continent. In some highly arid areas (parts of Alexander Island, the dry valleys of Victoria Land), the plant biomass is mostly in lakes and pools. South of 60°S there are many examples of mosses and lichens with restricted distribution.

Only two vascular plants indigenous to Antarctica[16] occur sparsely in coastal areas of maritime Antarctica and south of 68°S in Marguerite Bay.

Antarctic freshwater lakes are home to several species of very rare mosses.[17] A unique feature of the vegetation in some parts of maritime Antarctica is the deep banks of moss peat, up to 3 yards (metres) in depth and several thousand years old, extremely vulnerable to human disturbances.[18]

Due to the fragility of terrestrial ecosystems in this extreme environment, their recovery from serious disturbance would take at least several decades. They will be subjected to heavy stress by increased tourism and any oil development or exploration.

Terrestrial Fauna

About 150 species have been identified in the region. The groups represented are protozoans, rotifers, nematodes, tardegrades, insects and mites. There are no land vertebrates. Very little is known about the role of these creatures in Antarctic ecosystems.

[16]*Deschampsia antarctica* and *Colobanthus quitensis*.
[17]*Bryum korotkevitzae* from lakes in the Bunger Hills, *Plagiothecium siminovii* from lakes in the Schirmachervatna, and *Drepanocladus aduncus* in lakes on Signy Island and at Ablation Point.
[18]These are formed by *Chorisodontium aciphyllum* and *Polytrichum alpestre*.

Who Controls Antarctica?

Antartica has never been settled and does not appear conducive to largescale permanent settlement, yet it became the object of conventional territorial claims during the first half of the century. These claims are shown on the map.

The Antarctic Treaty   The *Antarctic Treaty* provides the primary legal framework for decision-making in the region. It was signed in 1959 by twelve countries with an active interest in Antarctica, and entered into force in 1961.[1] The Treaty resulted primarily from mutual scientific efforts of those nations during the International Geophysical Year (1957-58). It was seen initially as a device to defuse competition over the region, especially military competition, and to defer the question of sovereignty.

Seven nations had lodged claims by the time the Antarctic Treaty was signed in 1959[2], while a number of other countries, led by the US and USSR, expressly declined either to make their own claims or to recognize those made by others.[3]

The treaty establishes two categories of membership: full voting members (called *Consultative Parties*) include the twelve original signatories plus other countries actively involved in Antarctica through a serious scientific program. Poland joined the *Consultative Parties* in 1977 and West Germany was accepted as a full member in 1981.

Acceding parties cannot vote, and are not invited to the biennial meetings. They promise to abide by the Treaty's provisions and such agreed measures as the *Consultative Parties* develop for protection of the environment.

The voting parties to the agreement meet together every two years. They talk about matters of common interest and agree on measures and recommendations to carry out objectives of the Treaty. Recommendations adopted at consultative meetings become legally binding when approved by all governments. Recommendations cover a wide range of activities including telecommunications, tourism and protection of the environment.

The Treaty says Antarctica shall be used for peaceful purposes only. No military bases may be established there. Nuclear explosions in Antarctica and the disposal of radioactive wastes are prohibited.

---

[1] The text is reproduced in Appendix A.
[2] United Kingdom, Norway, Australia, New Zealand, Argentina, Chile.
[3] US, USSR, Belgium, Japan, South Africa. Poland and the Federal Republic of Germany, the newest members, also are non-claimants.

This disarmament regime is the only one specifically providing for on-site inspection. Since 1961 no evidence has come to light of military activities regarded by governments as inconsistent with the Treaty. These provisions, however, have not stopped member governments from staffing their scientific stations with military personnel. Argentina calls its stations 'military bases'.

The United States was not deterred from building a nuclear power reactor at McMurdo in the 1960s. When it was finally shut down in 1972 after years of problems and accidents, thousands of cubic metres of contaminated earth had to be removed.

One of the Treaty's main goals is to allow scientific research to be conducted in the region without regard to claims of sovereignty. Freedom of access to the entire continent is guaranteed. The co-operative spirit of scientific investigation developed during the International Geophysical Year (IGY) has been continued. The Treaty provides for the exchange of scientific information and personnel. Although there are often delays of several years while research data is tabulated, analysed and published, by and large these obligations have been observed. This may change, however, given the new interest in oil and other minerals. Several nations are conducting or planning 'research' of direct relevance to exploitation. Most likely they will want to keep the data for themselves.

The scope of scientific endeavour in Antarctica is quite broad, covering glaciology, biology, earth sciences, atmospheric sciences, ocean studies and biomedical research. To protect their legal and political positions in the region most parties have conducted significant scientific research programs.

The primary obstacle to the Treaty's continued vitality is the existence of various commercial resources, none covered expressly by the 1959 Treaty. These commercial developments are of utmost concern to conservationists and environmentalists.

Area

The Antarctic Treaty covers the entire area south of 60°S latitude. It includes the continental shelf and large land masses submerged by the weight of the ice covering; areas of the ocean that are 'high seas' regardless of how the territorial claims are resolved; areas that could be 200 mile (333 kilometre) exclusive economic zones if national sovereignty were to be implemented in the various claims; and areas which are part of 200 mile (333 kilometre) zones around certain islands owned by various nations.

Expiration

The Treaty has no expiration date. It could remain in force indefinitely. A 'review' is possible after 1991, however, if any consultative party requires it. If there was a review, changes could be made to the basic arrangements, including methods of decision-making, the nature of the Parties' control over the region, and activities covered.

The Question of Claims

Article IV of the Treaty sets out the compromise allowing differences between claimants and non-claimants to be put aside for the time being. Article IV states that signing the Treaty does not change a nation's legal position concerning claims of territorial sovereignty. Any activity conducted by the parties while the Treaty is in effect may not be used to assert, support or deny a claim. At least that is the theory. Some member nations have gone to great lengths to demonstrate their control of a claimed area. Argentina has arranged for births and marriages to take place on their bases and uses a visa system to control access to their claimed zone.

When the Antarctic Treaty was negotiated in 1959, questions of potential resource exploitation were not covered, as no country was particularly interested in such activities (other than whaling). To deal with resource ownership would have raised political difficulties between claimants and non-claimants virtually impossible to resolve.

As the Treaty is interpreted by claimants, exploration for and exploitation of any resource is a right inherent in their 'sovereignty'. Claimants say they have agreed to allow scientific expeditions of other countries within their claimed territories as part of a deal. In exchange they receive similar access to the whole continent by their nationals, scientific information, and mutually agreed restraints on certain activities by all parties.

Non-claimants defend their exploration and exploitation activities as a permitted 'peaceful use' of the area under Article I. They say no nation has territorial sovereignty, the marine areas off the coast are entirely 'high seas', and no territorial seas or 200 mile (333 kilometre) economic zones exist. As for oil and other minerals, non-claimants say any attempt by a claimant nation to enforce its 'sovereignty' to interfere with a peaceful activity by another Treaty party would be a breach of the Treaty.

So far there has been no direct conflict, because all governments have voluntarily agreed to limit their activities. But some nations now are beginning oil and mineral exploration.

A problem is also posed by overlapping and conflicting claims, which are shown on the map.

There is a widely shared perception that both the United States and USSR would file their own claims to large portions of the continent if compromises embodied in the Treaty were to break down. This could happen if claimant nations began acting to exercise their 'sovereignty'.

Treatment of Environmental Protection and Conservation Issues in the Antarctic

The Treaty Parties have devoted substantial efforts during the last twenty years to protecting the environment. They have drawn up a set of 'Agreed Measures for the Conservation of Fauna and Flora', set aside several specially protected areas, and developed environmental guidelines for tourists (Appendix B).

In 1972 a Convention on Antarctic Seals was negotiated, with jurisdiction out to the limits of the Antarctic Treaty, 60°S latitude. This agreement has not been seriously tested because no nation has indicated a serious desire to harvest seals commercially (Appendix C).

In 1980 the Consultative Parties, joined by the Federal Republic of Germany and the German Democratic Republic, completed the Convention on the Conservation of Antarctic Marine Living Resources (Appendix D). This Convention contains an innovative concept, the 'ecosystem approach', a biological model which attempts to consider the effects of exploitation of one species on all other species in the Antarctic ecosystem.

This demonstrates that the consultative parties are aware of environmental, conservation and political issues posed by resource exploitation.

But many have criticized the Marine Living Resources Convention, primarily because of its consensus decision-making requirement and failure to face directly the need for national quotas. Nations involved have not provided the funding or the research necessary to allow the Convention to be properly implemented, nor is it clear how critical issues such as rules of procedure for the scientific committee will be handled.

Basically, the Antarctic Treaty Consultative Parties have developed a decent *framework* for protecting the environment. But this has been done without the existence of substantial pressures for commercial development and exploitation. It is those pressures which worry conservation and environmental organizations.

The *secrecy* of the Antarctic Treaty meetings is one of the most troubling problems to conservation and environmental organizations. The Parties keep their decisions to themselves. Some of the worrying aspects of that secrecy are:

- no observers are permitted at meetings of the Parties;
- reports of meetings are sometimes misleading, and critical information is often omitted;
- little effort is made to seek views or advice from other interested governments or organizations. Drafts of Treaty texts are not circulated to experts or interested organizations;
- few delegations contain public members;
- representatives of governments that have acceded to the Treaty are not allowed to attend.

What is Going On in Antarctica?

Introduction

The principal activities of concern are:

a. oil and mineral exploration;
b. commercial oil drilling or mining;
c. excessive krill or finfish harvests; and
d. seal and penguin industries.

It is impossible at present to evaluate impacts from even relatively modest exploitation of either living or mineral resources in the region. Present technology is clearly insufficient to minimize properly risks of oil exploitation.

Environmental interests would be best served if the Antarctic region continues to be a free scientific zone not appreciably affected by modern commercial development or exploitation. This way, it could continue to be a key monitoring zone for global pollution, a scientific preserve for wide-ranging research of interest to all humans and a safe habitat for the largest populations of wildlife on the planet.

A long-term moratorium on commercial exploration and exploitation of oil and other minerals, and a krill fishery designed as a long-term scientific experiment could accomplish the desired result, for the time being.

The best solution would be an international agreement to protect fully Antarctica from all mineral activities. This could be accomplished by modifying the existing Antarctic Treaty, or through the United Nations.

Among the approaches that have been discussed are a World Park, Global Preserve or Heritage Monument. The Antarctic Treaty nations could also act as trustees for the rest of the world to protect the region. It is not the name that matters. The important thing is what activities are to be prohibited.

The Question of Oil and Minerals

The Treaty Parties and various scientific organizations are conducting scientific research related to the mineral potential of the continent and offshore areas.

Commercial exploration and expoitation activities have been 'voluntarily' prohibited for several years, although there is a fine line between geophysical 'scientific research' and 'commercial' oil exploration. (The voluntary restraint policy is explained in Appendix F.)

Some nations and oil companies apparently believe enough is now known to drill safe exploratory wells!

The Consultative Parties will convene a special series of negotiations during the next few years to try and develop a mutually agreed solution to the mineral question. These will be closed to all other nations and organizations.

There is no indication that any government is now willing to propose the 'full protection' option of closing Antarctica to mineral exploitation, either for a stated period, or for all time.

Any Antarctic minerals regime is of great importance to environmental and conservation organizations because it will affect their interests in the region.

During the next few years, environmental and conservation organizations need to pursue parallel paths. They must raise public awareness about values in the region and the consequences of minerals exploitation, with the goal of fully protecting the Antarctic. They must also work *with* the Antarctic Treaty Consultative Parties to ensure that *if* a mineral regime is developed, it is environmentally sound.

It became apparent petroleum could be extracted from the Antarctic when *Glomar Challenger* drilled four holes in the Ross Sea continental shelf in 1972, finding traces of hydrocarbons.

Likelihood of Oil in Antarctica

Comparisons with existing oil-bearing strata in the southern-most parts of continents surrounding Antarctica make it possible to speculate on the likelihood of oil. The most interesting areas are the continental shelves of the Ross, Amundsen and Bellinghausen Seas and the continental shelf under the Weddell Sea. Analysts in the United States Geological Survey estimated in 1974 accessible continental shelves could contain 45,000 million barrels of oil. An estimate from Gulf Oil in 1979 was '50,000 million barrels and probably much more'.

In the Australian oil field, Bass Strait, estimates for probable amounts of oil are 3000 million barrels. Although this seems a lot less than the projected reserves recoverable in Antarctica, it must be borne in mind that, owing to the difficulties of exploration and exploitation in Antarctica, there may need to be significantly more oil available than at Bass Strait.

The seismic programmes will provide much better information. Would the field be large enough to compensate for the difficult conditions? All we know is that the oil companies are interested.

The first stage in serious exploration began in 1981 with a sophisticated seismic survey by the Japan National Oil Corporation to evaluate petroleum potential in the Bellinghausen Sea. Other governments have also done seismic work in recent years, and a number of oil companies have submitted proposals for commercial seismic projects. To date these proposals have been deferred by governments, but pressure for the seismic work to be allowed is growing.

A senior advisor to companies on international oil exploration has described the region's conditions as follows:

Dangers from Oil Drilling

Ice-chocked and stormy seas hinder access to the continent. Great cyclonic storms circle Antarctica in endless west-to-east procession. Moist maritime air interacting with cold polar air makes the Antarctic Ocean in the vicinity of the Polar Front one of the world's stormiest. The seas around Antarctica have often been likened to the moat surrounding a fortress. The turbulent 'roaring forties', 'furious fifties', and 'shrieking sixties' lie in a circumpolar storm track and a westerly oceanic current zone known commonly as the West Wind Drift, or Circumpolar Current. No lands break the relentless force of the prevailing west winds as they race clockwise around the continent, dragging westerly ocean currents along beneath. Superstructure icing can be expected offshore in all seasons.[1]

All exploratory drilling would be dangerous. If a blowout were not controlled by the end of the season it would be unchecked for at least another six months.

Production drilling and construction of pipelines and storage tanks would have more significant impact. In addition to continuing high risk of a blowout, there would be severe hazards for required oil tankers. Oil would be shipped out in large supertankers. Although such ships would have sufficient ice-breaking ability to operate year round, the risk of a shipping accident would be considerable.

A large labour force will be necessary to build and operate drilling rigs and new facilities on land will be required to support them. There is very little ice-free land along the coast not already occupied by birds or scientific bases. Disturbance and contamination of hundreds of square kilometres for accommodation, recreation and storage and related facilities would permanently damage those areas.

There will be inevitable pollution of adjacent coastal areas. Dust and pollution from these activities could alter the *albedo* (reflectance) leading to unpredictable and perhaps catastrophic changes in regional and global climate.

The largest oil spill from a tanker was 150,000 tons (*Amoco Cadiz* in 1978).

In the Antarctic, however, the consequences of an accident could be much greater because of the size of the tankers required to make the journey worthwhile (probably 500,000 tonnes) and the presence of huge icebergs. Salvage operations and clean up would be virtually impossible.

The release of a cargo of oil into the Ross Sea could adversely affect perhaps 1 million square kilometres.

Negative effects of oil on Antarctic organisms are known only in the most general respect.

- There is virtually no information on the tolerance of Antarctic species to oil slicks or petroleum accumulations that may collect on the sea floor, or long-term sub-lethal exposure to oil.
- The Ross Sea gyre makes it likely an oil slick persisting for a matter of months could become distributed along the coast of Victoria Land, with wide-spread impacts on coastal life, particularly sea birds and seals.
- Algae attached to pack ice is estimated to contribute up to 20 per cent of total primary production in the Antarctic seas, and could be of critical importance to many species at particular stages of their life cycle. A spill which spread under the sea ice would contaminate this community; nothing is known about its responses.
- Virtually nothing is known about feeding areas at sea of penguins and other seabirds.
- A shipping accident could change regional climate due to the impact of the oil slick on sea ice formation.
- Returning Antarctic waters to their natural state after a major spill would be impossible. The logistics of a clean-up would present severe problems because of the large area, its remoteness and the probable absence of extensive base facilities. Cleaning up a major oil spill to an 'acceptable'

[1] L F Ivanhoe, Novum Corp. (*Oil and Gas Journal*, 29 December, 1980).

degree would be difficult. *Natural breakdown of bacteria is between one and ten per cent of the rate for oil in the middle and low latitudes, because of the low temperatures.*

• If oil is associated with pack ice it will be impossible to separate and dispose of, and may become incorporated into the ice, depending on the time of year.

Governments should think twice before exposing Antarctica to such exploration and exploitation.

In response to a request from the Antarctic Treaty nations, a SCAR group of specialists[2] prepared a report on the *Possible Environmental Effects of Mineral Resource Exploration and Exploitation in Antarctica.*

Role of Scientific Committee on Antarctic Research (SCAR)

This was considered at the 9th and 10th Antarctic Treaty Consultative Meetings.

The report:

a. reviews present knowledge of mineral occurrences and resources in Antarctica;

b. identifies most likely areas for onshore and offshore exploration and exploitation; and

c. evaluates sensitivity of the Antarctic marine and terrestrial ecosystems to different environmental disturbances.

In response to SCAR and Antarctic Treaty Nations' request for further development of the study, the United States Polar Research Board arranged for an international workshop, held in Bellagio, Italy, 5-8 March 1979. The workshop explored likely locations and technical natures of Antarctic mineral exploration and exploitation and examined how such development might affect the environment. The workshop report, *Oil and Other Minerals in the Antarctic*, was published by SCAR.

Both reports were used to provide a scientific basis for discussion on Antarctic mineral resources during the 10th and 11th Consultative Meetings. They contain excellent summaries of the environmental unknowns and problems associated with any mineral activities in Antarctica.

The Bellagio report on environmental implications of possible mineral exploitation stressed Antarctica should be maintained as a unique scientific, political and environmental asset.

Environmentalists and conservationists are concerned about the impacts of harvesting marine life in the Antarctic on the target species themselves, and the implications of such catches on other dependent species. There already have been significant changes in the ecosystem caused by the radical depletion of whales over the last 100 years. An improperly managed Southern Ocean fishery, particularly for krill, may harm not only krill stocks, but the structure and dynamic interactions of the whole Antartic marine ecosystem.

Commercial Harvest of Fish, Krill, Seals and Penguins

IUCN, the International Institute of Environment and Development, and ASOC, all have petitioned the Treaty governments during the last few years

[2]This is the EAMREA (Environmental Impact Assessment of Mineral Resource Exploration and Exploitation in Antarctica) group, chaired by Dr James Zumberg.

to consider their proposals for managing the living resources of the Southern Ocean. However, no non-governmental organization was allowed to participate formally in the negotiations for the 'Ecosystem' Convention. Very few of the suggestions for improvements to the Convention were seriously considered by the governments.

For example, IUCN called on the governments in 1978 to delay any exploitation of living resources there until sound scientific data is available for management on a sustainable basis. All the environmental and conservation groups have urged that interim quotas be agreed for various areas in the Southern Ocean, which would stay in effect until changed by order of the new Southern Ocean Commission. All of these non-governmental groups have proposed that some areas be set aside from the beginning, free from any harvesting, and that a serious long term research programme be immediately undertaken. Their view is that the ecosystem should be understood before it is exploited further. The environmentalists have stressed the importance of an independent observer system, to ensure that rules are being followed, and have criticized the absence of central method for enforcement. The environmental community around the world has asked governments to pool all available information on the workings of the Antarctic marine ecosystem in a central data bank. Governments have so far ignored all of these suggestions and requests. Only time will tell, but there is no clear process for obtaining the necessary scientific information, or for providing independent scientific advice to the Commission and governments. The way the Commission is being structured and staffed, there will be no means for public accountability. Management decisions will be taken behind closed doors.

As for seals and penguins, environmental and conservation organizations are firm in their conviction that these animals should not be killed for commercial use. It has taken almost a century for the seals to recover from the last attack of humans. Penguins have never been killed in large quantities. They are symbol to most people of the special nature of the Antarctic.

Recommendation of Second World Conference on National Parks

In 1972 representatives from over eighty countries met at Grand Teton National Park in the United States to consider how to advance worldwide the national park concept. IUCN was a key co-sponsor of the conference; UNESCO and FAO also participated actively.

Governments were called on to establish Antarctica as a World Park under the auspices of the United Nations (see Appendix G for the text).

Following up this recommendation in 1975, New Zealand proposed that the Consultative Parties give Antarctica international park status, indicating a willingness to drop its own territorial claim. Other Antarctic Treaty Parties have never responded formally to the recommendation and New Zealand has withdrawn its proposal.

The recommendation has even more validity now. Every year we learn more about Antarctica's unique position and possible uses. Every year the dangers of commercial resource exploitation draw nearer.

The World Park proposal is being renewed at the Third World Conference in Bali, 1982. The World Park will only become a reality if people everywhere support the concept. Changing the minds of governments and multi-national companies will not be easy. The battle will not be won overnight. But it *is* possible for Antarctica to be protected from oil and mineral developments. It is possible for Antarctica to be the first World Park.

IUCN passed a major resolution in 1981 (see Appendix I). This follows several years of work by IUCN and WWF, including one section of the World Conservation Strategy (see Appendix G). These organizations will undertake a three year campaign to educate the public about Antarctic issues.

An important product of IUCN's campaign will be an *Antarctic Conservation Strategy*. Ideas from scientists and people world-wide are needed to make this as complete and specific as possible.

Because IUCN has been given observer status to the Marine Living Resources Commission and Scientific Committee, it is in a key position to raise important scientific and ecological issues.

IUCN Resolution of the General Assembly, Christchurch, New Zealand, 1981

On the tenth anniversary of the Stockholm Conference, environmentalists and conservationists from all over the world gathered in Nairobi, to review a decade's progress and make plans for the future. A resolution was passed regarding the future of Antarctica. It calls upon the Antarctic Treaty nations and the United Nations to consider making Antarctica a world park, in recognition of its status as a global commons. The text is in Appendix J.

Nairobi Resolution, 1982

SECTION 4

What Can You Do to Help Save Antarctica?

Become informed about the issues. Get a copy of the IIED Report (International Institute for Environment and Development) titled 'The Management of the Southern Ocean'. Get a copy of the Bellagio and SCAR-EAMREA reports from your Government or ASOC. Ask ASOC and The Antarctica Project for their materials. Check out your World Wildlife Fund office or other ASOC member organizations and try to co-ordinate your efforts with their strategies.[1] Antarctic environmental issues are complicated — add the political considerations and you have quite a mixture.

Become active. You can write, as an individual, to your Government and the United Nations, but organized efforts will be more productive. Circulate petitions for the World Park (see Appendix T) and send them to your Legislature or Parliament. Please send copies of all completed petitions to ASOC and the Antarctica Project.

- Urge your Government to work for Antarctica to be declared a *World Park* or Preserve, protecting this unique region from all oil and mineral activities.
- Call upon your Government to ensure that the world's first 'ecosystem' conservation regime for fishing is properly implemented. *In particular, demand that nothing be done in Antarctica that further harms endangered and threatened whales*.
- If your Government is not a full Consultative Party to the Antarctic Treaty, work to have your diplomats raise the issues in the United Nations.
- If your government has acceded to the Antarctic Treaty but is not a full voting member, urge your officials to request the right to attend all minerals negotiations, and other Antarctic meetings.
- If your Government is a full Consultative Party to the Antarctic Treaty, urge that IUCN, ASOC and other observers be allowed to participate in mineral negotiations, and other Antarctic meetings.
- Urge your Government to stop the *secrecy* of Antarctic meetings.
- Circulate petitions to schools, churches, societies, clubs and other organizations and send them to your Legislature or Parliament. Please send copies to ASOC and the Antarctica Project.
- Get sympathetic politicians, lawmakers and party leaders to hold inquiries or hearings on your Government's position on Antarctica.
- Ask your local politicians where they stand on the issue. Publicize those views.

[1]A list of ASOC's member organizations is in Appendix P.

- Organize a people's committee to work towards Antarctica being declared a World Park.
- Work with television, radio, newspapers and magazines to make the facts and issues known about the likely results of oil and mineral exploitation, and full-scale commercial fishing for krill.
- Write letters to local newspapers and articles for magazines.
- Discuss Antarctica on talk back radio. See if you can do a programme on public access radio or television.
- Show films about Antarctica on television and at schools.
- Approach your Government's education department and see if Antarctic issues can be included in the school curriculum.
- Petition the United Nations. Work to have the issues raised there and in other international forums.
- Have T-shirts, bumper bar stickers and badges made to support the cause. These items can also be obtained from ASOC and The Antarctica Project.
- Set up stalls giving information at local schools, universities, markets and shopping centres.
- Develop alliances with IUCN, World Wildlife Fund, ASOC and other organizations so that world-wide lobbies can be maintained.
- Appoint one person in your group to liaise with ASOC and with the International Steering Committee being formed by the Antarctica Project.
- Join the Antarctica Project. Become a 'Friend of Antarctica'.

ASOC, IUCN, The Antarctica Project and World Wildlife Fund will all be producing materials useful to any campaigns.

Should you need help in planning your strategy, or need information, posters, films or photographs, write to these organizations.

Remember, Antarctica's future depends on you! Everyone can help.

Environmental organizations and groups in each country must develop an overall strategy pertinent to their own political situation. For example, a country which is a full member of the Antarctic Treaty must be approached in a different manner to a non-member country. Claimant nations are in a different position than non-claimants.

No effort should be spared in preserving Antarctica.

What has been done so far?

In 1979 and 1980, conservation and environmental organizations in the United States of America wrote to President Carter about Antarctica. They urged the President to consider the value of Antarctica as an internationally protected area before any efforts were made to negotiate a mineral treaty, and asked that the concept of a World Park be explored. This also occurred in Australia.

In 1981 members of ASOC wrote to the heads of each Antarctic Treaty Government about protecting Antarctica from mineral development. They also urged the Treaty Governments to consider the idea of a World Park. (A sample letter is contained in Appendix Q.) The governments ignored these requests, and are working actively for a new minerals treaty.

No government is yet supporting the option of full protection for Antarctica from mineral exploitation, nor is there governmental support for managing Antarctic fisheries as a long-term scientific experiment.

The real issue facing the world is: *Protection versus Exploitation.*

Unless a world-wide campaign in favour of protecting Antarctica is begun, it is inevitable that Governments will eventually develop a treaty allowing oil development.

The Consultative Parties will probably try to develop some method of sharing ownership of the region's minerals among themselves in the absence of initiatives from the United Nations. The Antarctic Treaty Consultative Parties carefully guard their assumed prerogatives over the region. Environmentalists believe the Parties intend to develop a minerals treaty secretly without the assistance or participation of anyone else. This would then be presented to the world as a *fait accompli*, just as the Marine Living Resources Convention was.

It is unlikely that any arrangement allowing minerals to be exploited would adequately protect the Antarctic environment.

What should our Environmental Objectives be during the next few Years?

Research is the key to understanding Antarctic ecosystems. Governments should be urged to support an International Decade of Southern Ocean Research.

A main component of the research programme would be BIOMASS (see Appendix H), which now is starved for funds. If the BIOMASS programme were fully funded, results may answer 80 percent of the answers needed for the 'ecosystem' Marine Living Resources Convention to function properly.

No Government apparently will voluntarily develop a long term research programme for the Southern Ocean.

Southern Ocean krill and finfish should be harvested *only* as part of a giant scientific experiment over the next twenty years or so. Ideally, this would involve assigning the new Scientific Committee[2] a substantial charter and powers involving the following actions:

a. Closing some areas to fishing immediately.
b. Evaluating the role and status of all finfish before mass exploitation.
c. Establishment of a comprehensive data bank.
d. Full provision of all data from fishing countries (including data from fishing during the last decade), on an agreed, standardized scientific basis.
e. Establishment of conservative initial quotas by area.
f. Control over pace and character of development of all fisheries.
g. Independence, proper funding and adequate staffing of the Scientific Committee.
h. Joint actions with the International Whaling Commission Scientific Committee to set up a new Committee on Southern Ocean Fisheries. This committee could organize studies on the impacts of various fishery levels on whales and other species.

This method of managing the fishery would provide information otherwise impossible to obtain, but it is unlikely this method will be chosen unless conservation and environmentalist groups press strongly for it.

---

[2]This Scientific Committee is created under the Marine Living Resources Convention. It is critical to efforts to protect species and ecosystems in the Southern Ocean.

The principal feeding grounds of threatened and endangered blue, fin, humpback and right whales must be identified and closed to krill fishing.

The great whales must not be starved to death now that the world has finally decided to stop killing them!

a. The Scientific Committee must have *open procedures* allowing participation of all interested organizations. Consensus decision making is *not* appropriate for the Scientific Committee.
b. ASOC and *other environmental organizations must be allowed observer status* at meetings of the Commission and Scientific Committee.
c. *Very low harvest quotas* for krill and finfish should be set initially, and all future increases in quotas must be based only on submission and analysis of adequate data, as part of the on-going *experimental* fishery. No fishing for krill should be allowed that could further harm threatened and endangered whales.
d. A centralized *inspection and enforcement programme* must be established to make sure the Convention is being honoured.
e. A *Technical Committee* should be established to review economic aspects of the fishery. This is to prevent over-capitalization, which would lead to improper quotas.
f. All countries fishing in the Southern Ocean should be invited to participate in the 'ecosystem' Convention, including Taiwan and South Korea.[3]
g. Contracting Parties must provide a *budget* that allows the Commission and Scientific Committee to carry out the conservation duties of Article II.
h. There must be a core group of scientifically trained personnel in the Secretariat. Staff size and skills should be based on a fair appraisal of aims, functions, and principles set forth in the Convention.

Any attempted resumption of commercial sealing should be blocked. The Japanese and Argentine proposals for killing penguins in the subantarctic islands should be objected to. The Antarctic region should be a true sanctuary where all forms of wildlife can live in their natural state, free from fear.

[3]Taiwan and South Korea have been blocked from being members of the new Commission for political reasons.

Conclusion

Antarctica and its surrounding oceans hold a unique place in the history of the world. Rich in animal, mineral and marine plant life, the region provides an opportunity for scientists, conservationists and environmentalists to understand the world's most extraordinary ecosystem.

Antarctica's role in relation to global environment, climate and weather is unknown but scientists agree it is critically important.

The foundation species of the entire Southern Ocean ecosystem, Antarctic krill, directly or indirectly supports all higher species, including whales, seals, penguins, seabirds, fish and squid.

Antarctica is the feeding ground for the great whales, now seriously endangered, and for a large number of other species of whales.

Millions of seals thrive in Antarctica and would be threatened by habitat destruction.

Birds, fish, squid and terrestrial vegetation are all under threat from oil and mineral exploration and exploitation.

The world's first 'ecosystem' based fishing treaty, the Convention on the Conservation of Antarctic Marine Living Resources, provides an opportunity to deal constructively with environmental, conservation and political issues posed by exploitation of living resources. But concerned people who want to save Antarctica must ensure that their Governments fund, implement and enforce this Convention.

If Antarctica is exposed to mineral and oil exploitation, or excess harvesting of krill and finfish, the disastrous results could be irreversible.

Conservationists and environmentalists world-wide are uniting in their goal of ensuring that Antarctica will be protected forever. A world-wide movement will lobby governments everywhere to declare Antarctica a World Park. It will also work for greatly increased research of the region, in order to provide a better understanding of this special place.

There has never been a more urgent need for people to stand up and declare their intention to protect this extraordinary region. Antarctica can become a symbol of hope to all people, a living reminder of human ability to preserve its past, present and future, and to live in harmony with nature.

There will never be another Antarctica. Unless people act *NOW* it may be too late.

The efforts you make to save Antarctica underline *your* faith in our world's future. Antarctica is a legacy we can leave to ongoing generations for all time. It is a heritage that must be protected.

If Antarctica is saved, conservation, environmental, animal welfare groups and ordinary people all over the world will have won a victory no government can ignore. It will be a step forward toward saving Planet Earth.

Appendices

Appendices

Contents

Photographs on next 8 pages
1. Adelie penguins, Humble Island, Antarctic Peninsula, February 1976
2. Wiencke Island, Bismarck Strait, Antarctic Peninsula, February 1976
3. Fin whales blowing, Gerlache Strait, Antarctic Peninsula, February 1976
4. Humpbacked whale, Gerlache Strait, Antarctic Peninsula, February 1976
5. Chinstrap penguins, Couverville Island, Antarctic Peninsula, January 1975
6. Weddell seal with pup, Hutton Cliffs, Ross Island, December 1975
7. Iceberg, Amundsen Sea, Antarctica, January 1976
8. Killer whales, McMurdo Sound, Antarctica, December 1975
9. Elephant seal, Humble Island, Antarctic Peninsula
10. Antarctic Tern, Joubin Islands, Antarctic Peninsula, January 1975
11. Giant Fulmars, Litchfield Island, Antarctic Peninsula, January 1975
12. Blue-eyed Shags, Cormorant Island, Antarctic Peninsula, February 1976
13. Skuas, Litchfield Island, Antarctic Peninsula, February 1976

The Antarctic Treaty

The Governments of Argentina, Australia, Belgium, Chile, the French Republic, Japan, New Zealand, Norway, the Union of South Africa, the Union of Soviet Socialist Republics, the United Kingdom of Great Britain and Northern Ireland, and the United States of America;

Recognizing that it is in the interest of all mankind that Antarctica shall continue forever to be used exclusively for peaceful purposes and shall not become the scene or object of international discord;

Acknowledging the substantial contributions to scientific knowledge resulting from international cooperation in scientific investigation in Antarctica;

Convinced that the establishment of a firm foundation for the continuation and development of such cooperation on the basis of freedom of scientific investigation in Antarctica as applied during the International Geophysical Year accords with the interests of science and the progress of all mankind;

Convinced also that a treaty ensuring the use of Antarctica for peaceful purposes only and the continuance of international harmony in Antarctica will further the purposes and principles embodied in the Charter of the United Nations;

Have agreed as follows:

Article I

1. Antarctica shall be used for peaceful purposes only. There shall be prohibited, *inter alia*, any measures of a military nature, such as the establishment of military bases and fortifications, the carrying out of military manoeuvers, as well as the testing of any type of weapons.

2. The present Treaty shall not prevent the use of military personnel or equipment for scientific research or for any other peaceful purpose.

Article II

Freedom of scientific investigation in Antarctica and cooperation toward that end, as applied during the International Geophysical Year, shall continue, subject to the provisions of the persent Treaty.

Article III

1. In order to promote international cooperation in scientific investigation in Antarctica, as provided for in Article II of the present Treaty, the Contracting Parties agree that, to the greatest extent feasible and practicable:

a. information regarding plans for scientific programs in Antarctica shall be exchanged to permit maximum economy and efficiency of operations;

b. scientific personnel shall be exchanged in Antarctica between expeditions and stations;

c. scientific observations and results from Antarctica shall be exchanged and made freely available.

2. In implementing this Article, every encouragement shall be given to the establishment of cooperative working relations with those Specialized Agencies of the United Nations and other international organizations having a scientific or technical interest in Antarctica.

Article IV

1. Nothing contained in the present Treaty shall be interpreted as:

a. a renunciation by any Contracting Party of previously asserted rights of or claims to territorial sovereignty in Antarctica;

b. a renunciation or diminution by any Contracting Party of any basis of claim to territorial sovereignty in Antarctica which it may have whether as a result of its activities or those of its nationals in Antarctica, or otherwise;

c. prejudicing the position of any Contracting Party as regards its recognition or non-recognition of any other State's right of or claim or basis of claim to territorial sovereignty in Antarctica.

2. No acts or activities taking place while the present Treaty is in force shall constitute a basis for asserting, supporting or denying a claim to territorial sovereignty in Antarctica or create any rights of sovereignty in Antarctica. No new claim, or enlargement of an existing claim, to territorial sovereignty in Antarctica shall be asserted while the present Treaty is in force.

Article V

1. Any nuclear explosions in Antarctica and the disposal there of radioactive waste material shall be prohibited.

2. In the event of the conclusion of international agreements concerning the use of nuclear energy, including nuclear explosions and the disposal of radioactive waste material, to which all of the Contracting Parties whose representatives are entitled to participate in the meetings provided for under Article IX are parties, the rules established under such agreements shall apply in Antarctica.

Article VI

The provisions of the present Treaty shall apply to the area south of 60° South Latitude, including all ice shelves, but nothing in the present Treaty shall prejudice or in any way affect the rights, or the exercise of the rights, of any State under international law with regard to the high seas within that area.

Article VII

1. In order to promote the objectives and ensure the observance of the provisions of the present Treaty, each Contracting Party whose representatives are entitled to participate in the meetings referred to in Article IX of the Treaty shall have the right to designate observers to carry out any inspection provided for by the present Article. Observers shall be nationals of the Contracting Parties which designate them. The names of observers shall be communicated to every other Contracting Party having the right to designate observers, and like notice shall be given of the termination of their appointment.

2. Each observer designated in accordance with the provisions of paragraph 1 of this Article shall have complete freedom of access at any time to any or all areas of Antarctica.

3. All areas of Antarctica, including all stations, installations and equipment within those areas, and all ships and aircraft at points of discharging or embarking cargoes or personnel in Antarctica, shall be open at all time to inspection by any observers designated in accordance with paragraph 1 of this Article.

4. Aerial observation may be carried out at any time over any or all areas of Antarctica by any of the Contracting Parties having the right to designate observers.

5. Each Contracting Party shall, at the time when the present Treaty enters into force for it, inform the other Contracting Parties, and thereafter shall give them notice in advance, of

  a. all expeditions to and within Antarctica, on the part of its ships or nationals, and all expeditions to Antarctica organized in or proceeding from its territory;

  b. all stations in Antarctica occupied by its nationals; and

  c. any military personnel or equipment intended to be introduced by it into Antarctica subject to the conditions prescribed in paragraph 2 of Article I of the present Treaty.

Article VIII

1. In order to facilitate the exercise of their functions under the present Treaty, and without prejudice to the respective positions of the Contracting Parties relating to jurisdiction over all other persons in Antarctica, observers designated under paragraph 1 of Article VII and scientific personnel exchanged under subparagraph 1 (b) of Article III of the Treaty, and members of the staffs accompanying any such persons, shall be subject only to the jurisdiction of the Contracting Party of which they are nationals in respect of all acts or omissions occurring while they are in Antarctica for the purpose of exercising their functions.

2. Without prejudice to the provisions of paragraph 1 of this Article, and pending the adoption of measures in pursuance of subparagraph 1 (e) of Article IX, the Contracting Parties concerned in any case of dispute with regard to the exercise of jurisdiction in Antarctica shall immediately consult together with a view to reaching a mutually acceptable solution.

Article IX

1. Representatives of the Contracting Parties named in the preamble to the present Treaty shall meet at the City of Canberra within two months after the date of entry into force of the Treaty, and thereafter at suitable intervals and places, for the purpose of exchanging information, consulting together on matters of common interest pertaining to Antarctica, and formulating and considering, and recommending to their Governments, measures in furtherance of the principles and objectives of the Treaty, including measures regarding:

  a. use of Antarctica for peaceful purposes only;

  b. facilitation of scientific research in Antarctica;

  c. facilitation of international scientific cooperation in Antarctica;

  d. facilitation of the exercise of the rights of inspection provided for in Article VII of the Treaty;

  e. questions relating to the exercise of jurisdiction in Antarctica;

  f. preservation and conservation of living resources in Antarctica.

2. Each Contracting Party which has become a party to the present Treaty by accession under Article XIII shall be entitled to appoint representatives to participate in the meetings referred to in paragraph 1 of the present Article, during such time as that Contracting Party demonstrates its interest in Antarctica by conducting substantial scientific research activity there, such as the establishment of a scientific station or the despatch of a scientific expedition.

3. Reports from the observers referred to in Article VII of the present Treaty shall be transmitted to the representatives of the Contracting Parties participating in the meetings referred to in paragraph 1 of the present Article.

4. The measures referred to in paragraph 1 of this Article shall become effective when approved by all the Contracting Parties whose representatives were entitled to participate in the meetings held to consider those measures.

5. Any or all of the rights established in the present Treaty may be exercised as from the date of entry into force of the Treaty whether or not any measures facilitating the exercise of such rights have been proposed, considered or approved as provided in this Article.

Article X

Each of the Contracting Parties undertakes to exert appropriate efforts, consistent with the Charter of the United Nations, to the end that no one engages in any activity in Antarctica contrary to the principles or purposes of the present Treaty.

Article XI

1. If any dispute arises between two or more of the Contracting Parties concerning the interpretation or application of the present Treaty, those Contracting Parties shall consult among themselves with a view to having the dispute resolved by negotiation, inquiry, mediation, conciliation, arbitration, judicial settlement or other peaceful means of their own choice.

2. Any dispute of this character not so resolved shall, with the consent, in each case, of all parties to the dispute, be referred to the International Court of Justice for settlement; but failure

to reach agreement on reference to the International Court shall not absolve parties to the dispute from the responsibility of continuing to seek to resolve it by any of the various peaceful means referred to in paragraph 1 of this Article.

Article XII

1a. The present Treaty may be modified or amended at any time by unanimous agreement of the Contracting Parties whose representatives are entitled to participate in the meetings provided for under Article IX. Any such modification or amendment shall enter into force when the depositary Government has received notice from all such Contracting Parties that they have ratified it.

b. Such modification or amendment shall thereafter enter into force as to any other Contracting Party when notice of ratification by it has been received by the depositary Government. Any such Contracting Party from which no notice of ratification is received within a period of two years from the date of entry into force of the modification or amendment in accordance with the provisions of subparagraph 1 (a) of this Article shall be deemed to have withdrawn from the present Treaty on the date of the expiration of such period.

2a. If after the expiration of thirty years from the date of entry into force of the present Treaty, any of the Contracting Parties whose representatives are entitled to participate in the meetings provided for under Article IX so requests by a communication addressed to the depositary Government, a Conference of all the Contracting Parties shall be held as soon as practicable to review the operation of the Treaty.

b. Any modification or amendment to the present Treaty which is approved at such a Conference by a majority of the Contracting Parties there represented, including a majority of those whose representatives are entitled to participate in the meetings provided for under Article IX, shall be communicated by the depositary Government to all the Contracting Parties immediately after the termination of the Conference and shall enter into force in accordance with the provisions of paragraph 1 of the present Article.

c. If any such modification or amendment has not entered into force in accordance with the provisions of subparagraph 1 (a) of this Article within a period of two years after the date of its communication to all the Contracting Parties, any Contracting Party may at any time after the expiration of that period give notice to the depositary Government of its withdrawal from the present Treaty; and such withdrawal shall take effect two years after the receipt of the notice by the depositary Government.

Article XIII

1. The present Treaty shall be subject to ratification by the signatory States. It shall be open for accession by any State which is a Member of the United Nations, or by any other State which may be invited to accede to the Treaty with the consent of all the Contracting Parties whose representatives are entitled to participate in the meetings provided for under Article IX of the Treaty.

2. Ratification of or accession to the present Treaty shall be effected by each State in accordance with its constitutional processes.

3. Instruments of ratification and instruments of accession shall be deposited with the Government of the United States of America, hereby designated as the depositary Government.

4. The depositary Government shall inform all signatory and acceding States of the date of each deposit of an instrument of ratification or accession, and the date of entry into force of the Treaty and of any modification or amendment thereto.

5. Upon the deposit of instruments of ratification by all the signatory States, the present Treaty shall enter into force for those States and for States which have deposited instruments of accession. Thereafter the Treaty shall enter into force for any acceding State upon the deposit of its instrument of accession.

6. The present Treaty shall be registered by the depositary Government pursuant to Article 102 of the Charter of the United Nations.

Article XIV

The present Treaty, done in the English, French, Russian, and Spanish languages, each version being equally authentic, shall be deposited in the archives of the Government of the United States of America, which shall transmit duly certified copies thereof to the Governments of the signatory and acceding States.

In Witness Whereof, the undersigned Plenipotentiaries, duly authorized, have signed the present Treaty.

Done at Washington this first day of December one thousand nine hundred and fifty-nine.

[*Here follow the signatures of the Plenipotentiaries.*]

Agreed Measures for the Conservation of Antarctic Flora and Fauna

In 1964 the Agreed Measures for the Conservation of Flora and Fauna were drawn up. Though not yet ratified unanimously by the Consultative Parties, and therefore not binding, the Agreed Measures have been given legal effect as 'interim guidelines'.[1] They provide a basic structure of protection for all native species:

- The killing, wounding, capturing or molesting of any mammal or bird without a permit is forbidden. Permits, however, are issued unilaterally by each government with no consultation required.
- The Parties agree to 'minimize' harmful interferences with habitat, and to avoid pollution of inshore water.
- The concept of Specially Protected Areas is established in which even routine research, collection of species and use of vehicles is prohibited.
- The concept of Sites of Special Scientific Interest is established, requiring additional restrictions for some areas in order to protect their scientific potential.

1 Protection of Sites

The Agreed Measures have been carried out by regulations for the designation of 'Specially Protected Areas', 'Sites of Special Scientific Interest' and 'Marine Sites of Special Scientific Interest'. More than twenty areas have been so designated by mutual agreement of the Consultative Parties. SCAR has assisted the Parties in choosing appropriate sites and in developing management plans for them.

Recommendation VIII-3 established procedures for choosing and managing the sites. In general, the procedures developed are sound, and the Parties have been fairly responsive to proposals for protected status.

They have been most hesitant to act on proposed marine sites, perhaps because of a desire by some nations not to foreclose areas to future mineral exploitation.

2 General Recommendations

At the 1970 meeting the Treaty Parties agreed 'there is an increasingly urgent need to protect the environment from human interference', and stated they 'should assume responsibilities for the protection of the environment and the wise use of the Treaty Area'.

[1] Only Japan has not yet ratified these measures. Most of the Treaty Nations have already passed legislation to implement the agreed measures and now apply the rules to their own nationals.

In Recommendation VII-13, the Parties indicated their desire to act in Antarctica in accord with the interest of all humankind, to avoid modifying the environment, and to notify the international community of any changes that do occur.

At the 8th Consultative Meeting recommendations were agreed to on a Code of Conduct for Antarctic expeditions, waste disposal, (nuclear waste disposal was banned) and preparation by SCAR of environmental assessments of all major projects.

In Recommendation IX-5 adopted in 1977, the Parties stressed their desire to protect the Antarctic environment from harmful interference:

a. The Consultative Parties recognize their prime responsibility for the protection of the Antarctic environment from all forms of harmful human interference;

b. They will ensure in planning future activities, the question of environmental effects and the possible impact of such activities on the relevant ecosystems are duly considered;

c. They will refrain from activities having an inherent tendency to modify the Antarctic environment unless appropriate steps have been taken to foresee the probable modifications and to exercise appropriate controls with regard to harmful effects;

d. They will continue to monitor the Antarctic environment and to exercise their responsibility for informing the world community of any significant changes caused by human activities.

While the Parties' statements are strong, some have criticized them for inaction in alleviating local pollution, particularly around the major stations. Some scientists note that pollution from McMurdo Station, for example, is slowly changing the local environment. Meanwhile, big questions are looming on the horizon.

3 Tourism

One form of 'human interference' of concern during the past decade has been tourism.

The first formal Antarctic tourist activity was organized by the Chilean government in 1956. Cape Hallet was suggested as a possible site for a tourist hotel in the early 1960s. The Antarctic Peninsula was first visited by a tourist ship in 1965, the Lindblad Travel Company chartered *Lapataina*, an Argentine naval vessel. In 1967 Lindblad began to use a Danish vessel, *Magga Dan*, for Antarctic cruises. In January 1968, the ship ran aground in McMurdo Sound. Proposals were later put forward to use it as a floating hotel for tourists but these were never implemented. The *Magga Dan's* successor, the *Lindblad Explorer*, has undertaken many cruises in Antarctic waters, running aground twice, in 1972 and 1979.

Because of concerns about tourism, the United States' Navy declined permission for a 'Byrd Memorial' flight planned for December 1970 to land at McMurdo.

The first tourist-oriented flight to Antarctica was organized in November 1968 by the Richard E. Byrd Polar Center, of Boston. Tourist flights have been made in recent years over Antarctica, but have not landed. Both Air New Zealand and Qantas made several flights per season for a number of years, but the future of these flights is doubtful following the crash of an Air New Zealand DC10 on Mt Erebus in 1979, killing all aboard. Had there been survivors, Antarctic authorities would have been unable to recue the passengers in such a disaster.

In January 1981 the United States' Navy declined permission for an American expedition to make a private flight to Antarctica, partly because of the lack of support facilities. But such restrictions are the exception, and there is still no overall control over the continued development of tourism.

The Consultative Parties have attempted to ensure tourist visits are organized not to prejudice the conduct of scientific research or interfere with conservation of flora and fauna.

These measures include notification of all expeditions and visits of tourists, keeping visitors out of specially protected areas and ensuring all who enter the Treaty area are complying with 'Accepted Practices'.

Convention for the Conservation of Antarctic Seals

The Contracting Parties,

Recalling the Agreed Measures for the Conservation of Antarctic Fauna and Flora, adopted under the Antarctic Treaty signed at Washington on 1 December 1959;

Recognizing the general concern about the vulnerability of Antarctic seals to commercial exploration and the consequent need for effective conservation measures;

Recognizing that the stocks of Antarctic seals are an important living resource in the marine environment which requires an international agreement for its effective conservation;

Recognizing that this resource should not be depleted by over-exploitation, and hence that any harvesting should be regulated so as not to exceed the levels of the optimum sustainable yield;

Recognizing that in order to improve scientific knowledge and so place exploitation on a rational basis, every effort should be made both to encourage biological and other research on Antarctic seal populations and to gain information from such research from the statistics of future sealing operations, so that further suitable regulations may be formulated;

Noting that the Scientific Committee on Antarctic Research of the International Council of Scientific Unions (SCAR) is willing to carry out the tasks required of it in this Convention;

Desiring to promote and achieve the objectives of protection, scientific study and rational use of Antarctic seals, and to maintain a satisfactory balance within the ecological system,

Have agreed as follows:

Article 1 — Scope

1. This Convention applies to the seas south of 60° South Latitude, in respect of which the Contracting Parties affirm the provisions of Article IV of the Antarctic Treaty.

2. This Convention may be applicable to any or all of the following species:

Southern elephant seal *Mirounga leonina.*
Leopard seal *Hydrurga leptonyx.*
Weddell seal *Leptonychotes weddelli.*
Crabeater seal *Lobodon carcinophagus.*
Ross seal *Ommatophoca rossi.*
Southern fur seals *Arctocephalus* sp.

3. The Annex to this Convention forms an integral part thereof.

Article 2 — Implementation

1. The Contracting Parties agree that the species of seals enumerated in Article 1 shall not be killed or captured within the Convention area by their nationals or vessels under their respective flags except in accordance with the provisions of this Convention.

2. Each Contracting Party shall adopt for its nationals and for vessels under its flag such laws, regulations and other measures, including a permit system as appropriate, as may be necessary to implement this Convention.

Article 3 — Annexed Measures

1. This Convention includes an Annex specifying measures which the Contracting Parties hereby adopt. Contracting Parties may from time to time in the future adopt other measures with respect to the conservation, scientific study and rational and humane use of seal resources, prescribing *inter alia*:

a. permissible catch;

b. protected and unprotected species;

c. open and closed seasons;

d. open and closed areas, including the designation of reserves;

e. the designation of special areas where there shall be no disturbance of seals;

f. limits relating to sex, size, or age for each species;

g. restrictions relating to time of day and duration, limitations of effort and methods of sealing;

h. types and specifications of gear and apparatus and appliances which may be used;

i. catch returns and other statistical and biological records;

j. procedures for facilitating the review and assessment of scientific information;

k. other regulatory measures including an effective system of inspection.

2. The measures adopted under paragraph (1) of this Article shall be based upon the best scientfic and technical evidence available.

3. The Annex may from time to time be amended in accordance with the procedures provided for in Article 9.

Article 4 — Special Permits

1. Notwithstanding the provisions of this Convention, any Contracting Party may issue permits to kill or capture seals in limited quantities and in conformity with the objectives and principles of this Convention for the following purposes:

a. to provide indispensable food for men or dogs;

b. to provide for scientific research; or

c. to provide specimens for museums, educational or cultural institutions.

2. Each Contracting Party shall, as soon as possible, inform the other Contracting Parties and SCAR of the purpose ond content of all permits issued under paragraph (1) of this Article and subsequently of the numbers of seals killed or captured under these permits.

Article 5 — Exchange of Information and Scientific Advice

1. Each Contracting Party shall provide to the other Contracting Parties and to SCAR the information specified in the Annex within the period indicated therein.

2. Each Contracting Party shall also provide to the other Contracting Parties and to SCAR before 31 October each year information on any steps it has taken in accordance with Article 2 of this Convention during the preceding period 1 July to 30 June.

3. Contracting Parties which have no information to report under the two preceding paragraphs shall indicate this formally before 31 October each year.

4. SCAR is invited:

a. to assess information received pursuant to this Article; encourage exchange of scientific data and information among the Contracting Parties; recommend programmes for scientific research; recommend statistical and biological data to be collected by sealing expeditions within the Convention area; and suggest amendments to the Annex; and

b. to report on the basis of the statistical, biological and other evidence available when the harvest of any species of seal in the Convention area is having a significantly harmful effect on the total stocks of such species or on the ecological system in any particular locality.

5. SCAR is invited to notify the Depositary which shall report to the Contracting Parties when SCAR estimates in any sealing season that the permissable catch limits for any species are likely to be exceeded and, in that case, to provide an estimate of the date upon which the permissible catch limits will be reached. Each Contracting Party shall then take appropriate measures to prevent its nationals and vessels under its flag from killing or capturing seals of that species after the estimated date until the Contracting Parties decide otherwise.

6. SCAR may if necessary seek the technical assistance of the Food and Agriculture Organization of the United Nations in making its assessments.

7. Notwithstanding the provisions of paragraph (1) of Article 1 the Contracting Parties shall, in accordance with their internal law, report to each other and to SCAR, for consideration, statistics relating to the Antarctic seals listed in paragraph (2) of Article 1 which have been killed or captured by their nationals and vessels under their respective flags in the area of floating sea ice north of 60° South Latitude.

Article 6 — Consultations between Contracting Parties

1. At any time after commercial sealing has begun a Contracting Party may propose through the Depositary that a meeting of Contracting Parties be convened with a view to:

a. establishing by a two-thirds majority of the Contracting Parties, including the concurring votes of all States signatory to this Convention present at the meeting, an effective system of control, including inspection, over the implementation of the provisions of this Convention;

b. establishing a commission to perform such functions under this Convention as the Contracting Parties may deem necessary; or

c. considering other proposals, including:

i. the provision of independent scientific advice;

ii. the establishment, by a two-thirds majority, of a scientific advisory committee which may be assigned some or all of the functions requested of SCAR under this Convention, if commercial sealing reaches significant proportions;

iii. the carrying out of scientific programmes with the participation of the Contracting Parties; and

iv. the provision of further regulatory measures, including moratoria.

2. If one-third of the Contracting Parties indicate agreement the Depositary shall convene such a meeting, as soon as possible.

3. A meeting shall be held at the request of any Contracting Party, if SCAR reports that the harvest of any species of Antarctic seal in the area to which this Convention applies is having a significantly harmful effect on the total stocks of the ecological system in any particular locality.

Article 7 — Review of Operations

The Contracting Parties shall meet within five years after the entry into force of this Convention and at least every five years thereafter to review the operation of the Convention.

Article 8 — Amendments to the Convention

1. This Convention may be amended at any time. The text of any amendment proposed by a Contracting Party shall be submitted to the Depositary, which shall transmit it to all the Contracting Parties.

2. If one-third of the Contracting Parties request a meeting to discuss the proposed amendment the Depositary shall call such a meeting.

3. An amendment shall enter into force when the Depositary has received instruments of ratification or acceptance thereof from all the Contracting Parties.

Article 9 — Amendments to the Annex

1. Any Contracting Party may propose amendments to the Annex to this Convention. The text of any such proposed amendment shall be submitted to the Depositary which shall transmit it to all Contracting Parties.

2. Each such proposed amendment shall become effective for all Contracting Parties six months after the date appearing on the notification from the Depositary to the Contracting Parties, if within 120 days of the notification date, no objection has been received and two-thirds of the Contracting Parties have notified the Depositary in writing of their approval.

3. If an objection is received from any Contracting Party within 120 days of the notification date, the matter shall be considered by the Contracting Parties at their next meeting. If unanimity on the matter is not reached at the meeting, the Contracting Parties shall notify the Depositary within 120 days from the date of closure of the meeting of their approval or rejection of

the original amendment or of any new amendment proposed by the meeting. If, by the end of this period, two-thirds of the Contracting Parties have approved such amendment, it shall become effective six months from the date of the closure of the meeting for those Contracting Parties which have by then notified their approval.

4. Any Contracting Party which has objected to a proposed amendment may at any time withdraw that objection, and the proposed amendment shall become effective with respect to such Party immediately if the amendment is already in effect, or at such time as it becomes effective under the terms of this Article.

5. The Depositary shall notify each Contracting Party immediately upon receipt of each approval or objection, of each withdrawal of objection, and of the entry into force of any amendment.

6. Any State which becomes a party to this Convention after an amendment to the Annex has entered into force shall be bound by the Annex as so amended. Any State which becomes a Party to this Convention during the period when a proposed amendment is pending may approve or object to such an amendment within the time limits applicable to other Contracting Parties.

Article 10 — Signature
This Convention shall be open for signature at London from 1 June to 31 December 1972 by States participating in the Conference on the Conservation of Antarctic Seals held at London from 3 to 11 February 1972.

Article 11 — Ratification
This Convention is subject to ratification or acceptance. Instruments of ratification or acceptance shall be deposited with the Government of the United Kingdom of Great Britain and Northern Ireland, hereby designated as the Depositary.

Article 12 — Accession
This Convention shall be open for accession by any State which may be invited to accede to this Convention with the consent of all the Contracting Parties.

Article 13 — Entry into Force
1. This Convention shall enter into force on the thirtieth day following the date of deposit of the seventh instrument of ratification or acceptance.

2. Thereafter this Convention shall enter into force for each ratifying, accepting or acceding State on the thirtieth day after deposit by such State of its instrument of ratification, acceptance or accession.

Article 14 — Withdrawal
Any Contracting Party may withdraw from this Convention on 30 June of any year by giving notice on or before 1 January of the same year to the Depositary, which upon receipt of such a notice shall at once communicate it to the other Contracting Parties. Any other Contracting Party may, in like manner, within one month of the receipt of a copy of such a notice from the Depositary, give notice of withdrawal, so that the Con-

vention shall cease to be in force on 30 June of the same year with respect to the Contracting Party giving such notice.

Article 15 — Notifications by the Depositary
The Depositary shall notify all signatory and acceding States of the following:

a. signatures of this Convention, the deposit of instruments of ratification, acceptance or accession and notices of withdrawal;

b. the date of entry into force of this Convention and of any amendments to it or its Annex.

Article 16 — Certified Copies and Registration
1. This Convention, done in the English, French, Russian and Spanish languages, each version being equally authentic, shall be deposited in the archives of the Government of the United Kingdom of Great Britain and Northern Ireland, which shall transmit duly certified copies thereof to all signatory and acceding States.

2. This Convention shall be registered by the Depositary pursuant to Article 102 of the Charter of the United Nations.

IN WITNESS WHEREOF, the undersigned, duly authorized, have signed this Convention.

DONE at London, this 1st day of June 1972.

[Also in French Russian and Spanish.]

Annex
1. Permissible Catch
The Contracting Parties shall in any one year, which shall run from 1 July to 30 June inclusive, restrict the total number of seals of each species killed or captured to the numbers specified below. These numbers are subject to review in the light of scientific assessments:

a. in the case of crabeater seals *Lobodon carcinophagus*, 175,000;

b. in the case of Leopard seals *Hydrurgo leptonyx*, 12,000;

c. in the case of Weddell seals *Leptonychotes weddelli*, 5,000.

2. Protected Species
a. It is forbidden to kill or capture Ross seals *Ommatophoea rossi*, Southern elephant seals *Mirounga leonina*, or fur seals of the genus *Aretocephalis*.

b. In order to protect the adult breeding stock during the period when it is most concentrated and vulnerable, it is forbidden to kill or capture any Weddell seal *Leptonychotes weddelli* one year old or older between 1 September and 31 January inclusive.

3. Closed Season and Sealing Season
The period between 1 March and 31 August inclusive is a Closed Season, during which the killing or capturing of seals is forbidden. The period 1 September to the last day in February constitutes a Sealing Season.

4. Sealing Zones

Each of the sealing zones listed in this paragraph shall be closed in numerical sequence to all sealing operations for the seal species listed in paragraph 1 of this Annex for the period 1 September to the last day of February inclusive. Such closures shall begin with the same zone as is closed under paragraph 2 of Annex B to Annex 1 of the Report of the Fifth Antarctic Treaty Consultative Meeting at the moment the Convention enters into force. Upon the expiration of each closed period, the affected zone shall reopen:

Zone 1 — between 60° and 120° West Longitude

Zone 2 — between 0° and 60 ° West Longitude, together with that part of the Weddell Sea lying westward of 60° West Longitude

Zone 3 — between 0° and 70° East Longitude

Zone 4 — between 70° and 130° East Longitude

Zone 5 — between 130° East Longitude and 170° West Longitude

Zone 6 — between 120° and 170° West Longitude.

5. Seal Reserves

It is forbidden to kill or capture seals in the following reserves, which are seal breeding areas or the site of long-term scientific research;

a. The area around the South Orkney Islands between 60° 20′ and 60° 56′ South Latitude and 44° 05′ and 46° 25′ West Longitude.

b. The area of the southwestern Ross Sea south of 76° South Latitude and west of 170° East Longitude.

c. The area of Edisto Inlet south and west of a line drawn between Cape Hallet at 72° 19′ South Latitude, 170° 18′ East Longitude, and Helm Point, at 72° 11′ South Latitude, 170° 00′ East Longitude.

6. Exchange of Information

a. Contracting Parties shall provide before 31 October each year to other Contracting Parties and to SCAR a summary of statistical information on all seals killed or captured by their nationals and vessels under their respective flags in the Convention area, in respect of the preceding period 1 July to 30 June. This information shall include by zones and months:

i. The gross and nett tonnage, brake horse-power, number of crew, and number of days' operation of vessels under the flag of the Contracting Party;

ii. The number of adult individuals and pups of each species taken.

When specially requested, this information shall be provided in respect of each ship, together with its daily position at noon each operating day and the catch on that day.

b. When an industry has started, reports of the number of seals of each species killed or captured in each zone shall be made to SCAR in the form and at the intervals (not shorter than one week) requested by that body.

c. Contracting Parties shall provide to SCAR biological information, in particular:

i. Sex

ii. Reproductive condition

iii. Age

SCAR may request additional information or material with the approval of the Contracting Parties.

d. Contracting Parties shall provide to other Contracting Parties and to SCAR at least 30 days in advance of departure from their home ports, information on proposed sealing expeditions.

7. Sealing Methods

a. SCAR is invited to report on methods of sealing and to make recommendations with a view to ensuring that the killing or capturing of seals is quick, painless and efficient. Contracting Parties, as appropriate, shall adopt rules for their nationals and vessels under their respective flags engaged in the killing and capturing of seals, giving due consideration to the views of SCAR.

b. In the light of the available scientific and technical data, Contracting Parties agree to take appropriate steps to ensure that their nationals and vessels under their respective flags refrain from killing or capturing seals in the water, except in limited quantities to provide for scientific research in conformity with the objectives and principles of this Convention. Such research shall include studies as to the effectiveness of methods of sealing from the viewpoint of the management and humane and rational utilization of the Antarctic seal resources for conservation purposes. The undertaking and the results of any such scientific research programme shall be communicated to SCAR and the Depositary which shall transmit them to the Contracting Parties.

Convention on the Conservation of Antarctic Marine Living Resources

The Contracting Parties,

Recognizing the importance of safeguarding the environment and protecting the integrity of the ecosystem of the seas surrounding Antarctica;

Noting the concentration of marine living resources found in Antarctic waters and the increased interest in the possibilities offered by the utilization of these resources as a source of protein;

Conscious of the urgency of ensuring the conservation of Antarctic marine living resources;

Considering that it is essential to increase knowledge of the Antarctic marine ecosystem and its components so as to be able to base decisions on harvesting on sound scientific information;

Believing that the conservation of Antarctic marine living resources calls for international co-operation with due regard for the provisions of the Antarctic Treaty and with the active involvement of all States engaged in research or harvesting activities in Antarctic waters;

Recognizing the prime responsibilities of the Antarctic Treaty Consultative Parties for the protection and preservation of the Antarctic environment and, in particular, their responsibilities under Article IX, paragraph 1 (f) of the Antarctic Treaty in respect of the preservation and conservation of living resources in Antarctica;

Recalling the action already taken by the Antarctic Treaty Consultative Parties including in particular the Agreed Measures for the Conservation of Antarctic Fauna and Flora, as well as the provisions of the Convention for the Conservation of Antarctic Seals;

Bearing in mind the concern regarding the conservation of Antarctic marine living resources expressed by the Consultative Parties at the Ninth Consultative Meeting of the Antarctic Treaty and the importance of the provisions of Recommendation IX-2 which led to the establishment of the present Convention;

Believing that it is in the interest of all mankind to preserve the waters surrounding the Antarctic continent for peaceful purposes only and to prevent their becoming the scene or object of international discord;

Recognizing, in the light of the foregoing, that it is desirable to establish suitable machinery for recommending, promoting, deciding upon and co-ordinating the measures and scientific studies needed to ensure the conservation of Antarctic marine living organisms;

Have agreed as follows:

Article I

1. This Convention applies to the Antarctic marine living resources of the area south of 60° South latitude and to the Antarctic marine living resources of the area between that latitude and the Antarctic Convergence which form part of the Antarctic marine ecosystem.

2. Antarctic marine living resources means the populations of fin fish, molluscs, crustaceans and all other species of living organisms, including birds, found south of the Antarctic Convergence.

3. The Antarctic marine ecosystem means the complex of relationships of Antarctic marine living resources with each other and with their physical environment.

4. The Antarctic Convergence shall be deemed to be a line joining the following points along parallels of latitude and meridians of longitude:
50° S, 0°; 50° S, 30° E; 45° S, 30° E; 45° S, 80° E; 55° S, 80° E; 55° S, 150° E; 60° S, 150° E; 60° S, 50° W; 50° S, 50° W; 50° S, 0°.

Article II

1. The objective of this Convention is the conservation of Antarctic marine living resources.

2. For the purposes of this Convention, the term "conservation" includes rational use.

3. Any harvesting and associated activities in the area to which this Convention applies shall be conducted in accordance with the provisions of this Convention and with the following principles of conservation:

   a. prevention of decrease in the size of any harvested population to levels below those which ensure its stable recruitment. For this purpose its size should not be allowed to fall below a level close to that which ensures the greatest net annual increment;

   b. maintenance of the ecological relationships between harvested, dependent and related populations of Antarctic marine living resources and the restoration of depleted populations to the levels defined in sub-paragraph (a) above; and

   c. prevention of changes or minimization of the risk of changes in the marine ecosystem which are not potentially reversible over two or three decades, taking into account the state of available knowledge of the direct and indirect impact of harvesting, the effect of the introduction of alien species, the effects of associated activities on the marine ecosystem and of the effects of environmental changes, with the aim of making possible the sustained conservation of Antarctic marine living resources.

Article III

The Contracting Parties, whether or not they are Parties to the Antarctic Treaty, agree that they will not engage in any activities in the Antarctic Treaty area contrary to the principles and purposes of that Treaty and that, in their relations with each other, they are bound by the obligations contained in Articles I and V of the Antarctic Treaty.

Article IV

1. With respect to the Antarctic Treaty area, all Contracting Parties, whether or not they are Parties to the Antarctic Treaty, are bound by Articles IV and VI of the Antarctic Treaty in their relations with each other.
2. Nothing in this Convention and no acts or activities taking place while the present Convention is in force shall:
   a. constitute a basis for asserting, supporting or denying a claim to territorial sovereignty in the Antarctic Treaty area or create any rights of sovereignty in the Antarctic Treaty area;
   b. be interpreted as a renunciation or diminution by any Contracting Party of, or as prejudicing, any right of claim or basis of claim to exercise coastal state jurisdiction under international law within the area to which this Convention applies;
   c. be interpreted as prejudicing the position of any Contracting Party as regards its recognition or non-recognition of any such right, claim or basis of claim;
   d. affect the provision of Article IV, paragraph 2, of the Antarctic Treaty that no new claim, or enlargement of an existing claim, to territorial sovereignty in Antarctica shall be asserted while the Antarctic Treaty is on force.

Article V

1. The Contracting Parties which are not Parties to the Antarctic Treaty acknowledge the special obligations and responsibilities of the Antarctic Treaty Consultative Parties for the protection and preservation of the environment of the Antarctic Treaty area.
2. The Contracting Parties which are not Parties to the Antarctic Treaty agree that, in their activities in the Antarctic Treaty area, they will observe as and when appropriate the Agreed Measures for the Conservation of Antarctic Fauna and Flora and such other measures as have been recommended by the Antarctic Treaty Consultative Parties in fulfilment of their responsibility for the protection of the Antarctic environment from all forms of harmful human interference.
3. For the purposes of this Convention, "Antarctic Treaty Consultative Parties" means the Contracting Parties to the Antarctic Treaty whose Representatives participate in meetings under Article IX of the Antarctic Treaty.

Article VI

Nothing in this Convention shall derogate from the rights and obligations of Contracting Parties under the International Convention for the Regulation of Whaling and the Convention for the Conservation of Antarctic Seals.

Article VII

1. The Contracting Parties hereby establish and agree to maintain the Commission for the Conservation of Antarctic Marine Living Resources (hereinafter referred to as "the Commission").
2. Membership in the Commission shall be as follows:
   a. each Contracting Party which participated in the meeting at which this Convention was adopted shall be a Member of the Commission;
   b. each State Party which has acceded to this Convention pursuant to Article XXIX shall be entitled to be a Member of the Commission during such time as that acceding Party is engaged in research or harvesting activities in relation to the marine living resources to which this Convention applies;
   c. each regional economic integration organization which has acceded to this Convention pursuant to Article XXIX shall be entitled to be a Member of the Commission during such time as its States members are so entitled;
   d. a Contracting Party seeking to participate in the work of the Commission pursuant to sub-paragraphs (b) and (c) above shall notify the Depositary of the basis upon which it seeks to become a Member of the Commission and of its willingness to accept conservation measures in force. The Depositary shall communicate to each Member of the Commission such notification and accompanying information. Within two months of receipt of such communication from the Depositary, any Member of the Commission may request that a special meeting of the Commission be held to consider the matter. Upon receipt of such request, the Depositary shall call such a meeting. If there is no request for a meeting, the Contracting Party submitting the notification shall be deemed to have satisfied the requirements for Commission Membership.
3. Each Member of the Commission shall be represented by one representative who may be accompanied by alternate representatives and advisers.

Article VIII

The Commission shall have legal personality and shall enjoy in the territory of each of the States Parties such legal capacity as may be necessary to perform its function and achieve the purposes of this Convention. The privileges and immunities to be enjoyed by the Commission and its staff in the territory of a State Party shall be determined by agreement between the Commission and the State Party concerned.

Article IX

1. The function of the Commission shall be to give effect to the objective and principles set out in Article II of this Convention. To this end, it shall:
   a. facilitate research into and comprehensive studies of Antarctic marine living resources and of the Antarctic marine ecosystem;

b. compile data on the status of and changes in population of Antarctic marine living resources and on factors affecting the distribution, abundance and productivity of harvested species and dependent or related species or populations;

c. ensure the acquisition of catch and effort statistics on harvested populations;

d. analyse, disseminate and publish the information referred to in sub-paragraphs (b) and (c) above and the reports of the Scientific Committee;

e. identify conservation needs and analyse the effectiveness of conservation measures;

f. formulate, adopt and revise conservation measures on the basis of the best scientific evidence available, subject to the provisions of paragraph 5 of this Article;

g. implement the system of observation and inspection established under Article XXIV of this Convention;

h. carry out such other activities as are necessary to fulfil the objective of this Convention.

2. The conservation measures referred to in paragraph 1 (f) above include the following:

a. the designation of the quantity of any species which may be harvested in the area to which this Convention applies;

b. the designation of regions and sub-regions based on the distribution of populations of Antarctic marine living resources;

c. the designation of the quantity which may be harvested from the populations of regions and sub-regions;

d. the designation of protected species;

e. the designation of size, age and, as appropriate, sex of species which may be harvested;

f. the designation of open and closed seasons for harvesting;

g. the designation of the opening and closing of areas, regions or sub-regions for purposes of scientific study or conservation, including special areas for protection and scientific study;

h. regulation of the effort employed and methods of harvesting, including fishing gear, with a view, inter alia, to avoiding undue concentration of harvesting in any region or sub-region;

i. the taking of such other conservation measures as the Commission considers necessary for the fulfilment of the objective of this Convention, including measures concerning the effects of harvesting and associated activities on components of the marine ecosystem other than the harvested populations.

3. The Commission shall publish and maintain a record of all conservation measures in force.

4. In exercising its functions under paragraph 1 above, the Commission shall take full account of the recommendations and advice of the Scientific Committee.

5. The Commission shall take full account of any relevant measures or regulations established or recommended by the Consultative Meetings pursuant to Article IX of the Antarctic Treaty or by existing fisheries commissions responsible for species which may enter the area to which this Convention applies, in order that there shall be no inconsistency between the rights and obligations of a Contracting Party under such regulations or measures and conservation measures which may be adopted by the Commission.

6. Conservation measures adopted by the Commission in accordance with this Convention shall be implemented by Members of the Commission in the following manner:

a. the Commission shall notify conservation measures to all Members of the Commission;

b. conservation measures shall become binding upon all Members of the Commission 180 days after such notification, except as provided in sub-paragraphs (c) and (d) below;

c. If a Member of the Commission, within ninety days following the notification specified in sub-paragraph (a), notifies the Commission that it is unable to accept the conservation measure, in whole or in part, the measure shall not, to the extent stated, be binding upon that Member of the Commission;

d. in the event that any Member of the Commission invokes the procedure set forth in sub-paragraph (c) above, the Commission shall meet at the request of any Member of the Commission to review the conservation measure. At the time of such meeting and within thirty days following the meeting, any Member of the Commission shall have the right to declare that it is no longer able to accept the conservation measure, in which case the Member shall no longer be bound by such measure.

Article X

1. The Commission shall draw the attention of any State which is not a Party to this Convention to any activity undertaken by its nationals or vessels which, in the opinion of the Commission, affects the implementation of the objective of this Convention.

2. The Commission shall draw the attention of all Contracting Parties to any activity which, in the opinion of the Commission, affects the implementation by a Contracting Party of the objective of this Convention or the compliance by that Contracting Party with its obligations under this Convention.

Article XI

The Commission shall seek to co-operate with Contracting Parties which may exercise jurisdiction in marine areas adjacent to the area to which this Convention applies in respect of the conservation of any stock or stocks of associated species which occur both within those areas and the area to which this Convention applies, with a view to harmonizing the conservation measures adopted in respect of such stocks.

Article XII

1. Decisions of the Commission on matters of substance shall be taken by consensus. The question of whether a matter is one of substance shall be treated as a matter of substance.

2. Decisions on matters other than those referred to in paragraph 1 above shall be taken by a simple majority of the Members of the Commission present and voting.

3. In Commission consideration of any item requiring a decision, it shall be made clear whether a regional economic integration organization will participate in the taking of the decision and, if so, whether any of its member States will also participate. The number of Contracting Parties so participating shall not exceed the number of member States of the regional economic integration organization which are Members of the Commission.

4. In the taking of decisions pursuant to this Article, a regional economic integration organization shall have only one vote.

Article XIII

1. The headquarters of the Commission shall be established at Hobart, Tasmania, Australia.
2. The Commission shall hold a regular annual meeting. Other meetings shall also be held at the request of one-third of its members and as otherwise provided in this Convention. The first meeting of the Commission shall be held within three months of the entry into force of this Convention, provided that among the Contracting Parties there are at least two States conducting harvesting activities within the area to which this Convention applies. The first meeting shall, in any event, be held within one year of the entry into force of this Convention. The Depositary shall consult with the signatory States regarding the first Commission meeting, taking into account that a broad representation of such States is necessary for the effective operation of the Commission.
3. The Depositary shall convene the first meeting of the Commission at the headquarters of the Commission. Thereafter, meetings of the Commission shall be held at its headquarters, unless it decides otherwise.
4. The Commission shall elect from among its members a Chairman and Vice-Chairman, each of whom shall serve for a term of two years and shall be eligible for re-election for one additional term. The first Chairman shall, however, be elected for an initial term of three years. The Chairman and Vice-Chairman shall not be representatives of the same Contracting Party.
5. The Commission shall adopt and amend as necessary the rules of procedure for the conduct of its meetings, except with respect to the matters dealt with in Article XII of this Convention.
6. The Commission may establish such subsidiary bodies as are necessary for the performance of its functions.

Article XIV

1. The Contracting Parties hereby establish the Scientific Committee for the Conservation of Antarctic Marine Living Resources (hereinafter referred to as ''the Scientific Committee'') which shall be a consultative body to the Commission. The Scientific Committee shall normally meet at the headquarters of the Commission unless the Scientific Committee decides otherwise.
2. Each Member of the Commission shall be a member of the Scientific Committee and shall appoint a representative with suitable scientific qualifactions who may be accompanied by other experts and advisers.
3. The Scientific Committee may seek the advice of other scientists and experts as may be required on an ad hoc basis.

Article XV

1. The Scientific Committee shall provide a forum for consultation and co-operation concerning the collection, study and exchange of information with respect to the marine living resources to which this Convention applies. It shall encourage and promote co-operation in the field of scientific research in order to extend knowledge of the marine living resources of the Antarctic marine ecosystem.
2. The Scientific Committee shall conduct such activities as the Commission may direct in pursuance of the objective of this Convention and shall:
   a. establish criteria and methods to be used for determinations concerning the conservation measures referred to in Article IX of this Convention;
   b. regularly assess the status and trends of the populations of Antarctic marine living resources;
   c. analyse data concerning the direct and indirect effects of harvesting on the populations of Antarctic marine living resources;
   d. assess the effects of proposed changes in the methods or levels of harvesting and proposed conservation measures;
   e. transmit assessments, analyses, reports and recommendations to the Commission as requested or on its own initiative regarding measures and research to implement the objective of this Convention;
   f. formulate proposals for the conduct of international and national programs of research into Antarctic marine living resources.
3. In carrying out its functions, the Scientific Committee shall have regard to the work of other relevant technical and scientific organizations and to the scientific activities conducted within the framework of the Antarctic Treaty.

Article XVI

1. The first meeting of the Scientific Committee shall be held within three months of the first meeting of the Commission. The Scientific Committee shall meet thereafter as often as may be necessary to fulfil its functions.
2. The Scientific Committee shall adopt and amend as necessary its rules of procedure. The rules and any amendments thereto shall be approved by the Commission. The rules shall include procedures for the presentation of minority reports.
3. The Scientific Committee may establish, with the approval of the Commission, such subsidiary bodies as are necessary for the performance of its functions.

Article XVII

1. The Commission shall appoint an Executive Secretary to serve the Commission and Scientific Committee according to such procedures and on such terms and conditions as the Commission may determine. His term of office shall be for four years and he shall be eligible for re-appointment.
2. The Commission shall authorize such staff establishment for the Secretariat as may be necessary and the Executive Secretary shall appoint, direct and supervise such staff according to such rules, and procedures and on such terms and conditions as the Commission may determine.
3. The Executive Secretary and Secretariat shall perform the functions entrusted to them by the Commission.

Article XVIII

The official languages of the Commission and of the Scientific Committee shall be English, French, Russian and Spanish.

Article XIX

1. At each annual meeting, the Commission shall adopt by consensus its budget and the budget of the Scientific Committee.
2. A draft budget for the Commission and the Scientific Committee and any subsidiary bodies shall be prepared by the Executive Secretary and submitted to the Members of the Commission at least sixty days before the annual meeting of the Commission.
3. Each Member of the Commission shall contribute to the Budget. Until the expiration of five years after the entry into force of this Convention, the contribution of each Member of the Commission shall be equal. Thereafter the contribution shall be determined in accordance with two criteria: the amount harvested and an equal sharing among all Members of the Commission. The Commission shall determine by consensus the proportion in which these two criteria shall apply.
4. The financial activities of the Commission and Scientific Committee shall be conducted in accordance with financial regulations adopted by the Commission and shall be subject to an annual audit by external auditors selected by the Commission.
5. Each Member of the Commission shall meet its own expenses arising from attendance at meetings of the Commission and of the Scientific Committee.
6. A Member of the Commission that fails to pay its contributions for two consecutive years shall not, during the period of its default, have the right to participate in the taking of decisions in the Commission.

Article XX

1. The Members of the Commission shall, to the greatest extent possible, provide annually to the Commission and to the Scientific Committee such statistical, biological and other data and information as the Commission and Scientific Committee may require in the exercise of their functions.
2. The Members of the Commission shall provide, in the manner and at such intervals as may be prescribed, information about their harvesting activities, including fishing areas and vessels, so as to enable reliable catch and effort statistics to be compiled.
3. The Members of the Commission shall provide to the Commission at such intervals as may be prescribed information on steps taken to implement the conservation measures adopted by the Commission.
4. The Members of the Commission agree that in any of their harvesting activities, advantage shall be taken of opportunities to collect data needed to assess the impact of harvesting.

Article XXI

1. Each Contracting Party shall take appropriate measures within its competence to ensure compliance with the provisions of this Convention and with conservation measures adopted by the Commission to which the Party is bound in accordance with Article IX of this Convention.
2. Each Contracting Party shall transmit to the Commission information on measures taken pursuant to paragraph 1 above, including the imposition of sanctions for any violation.

Article XXII

1. Each Contracting Party undertakes to exert appropriate efforts, consistent with the Charter of the United Nations, to the end that no one engages in any activity contrary to the objective of this Convention.
2. Each Contracting Party shall notify the Commission of any such activity which comes to its attention.

Article XXIII

1. The Commission and the Scientific Committee shall co-operate with the Antarctic Treaty Consultative Parties on matters falling within the competence of the latter.
2. The Commission and the Scientific Committee shall co-operate, as appropriate, with the Food and Agriculture Organisation of the United Nations and with other Specialised Agencies.
3. The Commission and the Scientific Committee shall seek to develop co-operative working relationships, as appropriate, with inter-governmental and non-governmental organizations which could contribute to their work, including the Scientific Committee on Antarctic Research, the Scientific Committee on Oceanic Research and the International Whaling Commission.
4. The Commission may enter into agreements with the organizations referred to in this Article and with other organizations as may be appropriate. The Commission and the Scientific Committee may invite such organizations to send observers to their meetings and to meetings of their subsidiary bodies.

Article XXIV

1. In order to promote the objective and ensure observance of the provisions of this Convention, the Contracting Parties agree that a system of observation and inspection shall be established.
2. The system of observation and inspection shall be elaborated by the Commission on the basis of the following principles:
a. contracting Parties shall co-operate with each other to ensure the effective implementation of the system of observation and inspection, taking account of the existing international practice. This system shall include, inter alia, procedures for boarding and inspection by observers and inspectors designated by the Members of the Commission and procedures for flag state prosecution and sanctions on the basis of evidence resulting from such boarding and inspections. A report of such prosecutions and sanctions imposed shall be included in the information referred to in Article XXI of this Convention;
b. in order to verify compliance with measures adopted under this Convention, observation and inspection shall be carried out on board vessels engaged in scientific research or harvesting of marine living resources in the area to which this Convention applies, through observers and inspectors designated by the Members of the Commission and operating under terms and conditions to be established by the Commission;
c. designated observers and inspectors shall remain subject to the jurisdiction of the Contracting Party of which they are nationals. They shall report to the Member of the Commission by which they have been designated which in turn shall report to the Commission.

3. Pending the establishment of the system of observation and inspection, the Members of the Commission shall seek to establish interim arrangements to designate observers and inspectors and such designated observers and inspectors shall be entitled to carry out inspections in accordance with the principles set out in paragraph 2 above.

Article XXV

1. If any dispute arises between two or more of the Contracting Parties concerning the interpretation or application of this Convention, those Contracting Parties shall consult among themselves with a view to having the dispute resolved by negotiation, inquiry, mediation, conciliation, arbitration, judicial settlement or other peaceful means of their own choice.

2. Any dispute of this character not so resolved shall, with the consent in each case of all Parties to the dispute, be referred for settlement to the International Court of Justice or to arbitration; but failure to reach agreement on reference to the International Court or to arbitration shall not absolve Parties to the dispute from the responsibility of continuing to seek to resolve it by any of the various peaceful means referred to in paragraph 1 above.

3. In cases where the dispute is referred to arbitration, the arbitral tribunal shall be constituted as provided in the Annex to this Convention.

Article XXVI

1. This Convention shall be open for signature at Canberra from 1 August to 31 December 1980 by the States participating in the Conference on the Conservation of Antarctic Marine Living Resources held at Canberra from 7 to 20 May 1980.

2. The States which so sign will be the original signatory States of the Convention.

Article XXVII

1. This Convention is subject to ratification, acceptance or approval by signatory States.

2. Instruments of ratification, acceptance or approval shall be deposited with the Government of Australia, hereby designated as the Depositary.

Article XXVIII

1. This Convention shall enter into force on the thirtieth day following the date of deposit of the eighth instrument of ratification, acceptance or approval by States referred to in paragraph 1 of Article XXVI of this Convention.

2. With respect to each State or regional economic integration organization which subsequent to the date of entry into force of this Convention deposits an instrument of ratification, acceptance, approval or accession, the Convention shall enter into force on the thirtieth day following such deposit.

Article XXIX

1. This Convention shall be open for accession by any State interested in research or harvesting activities in relation to the marine living resources to which this Convention applies.

2. This Convention shall be open for accession by regional economic integration organizations constituted by sovereign States which include among their members one or more States Members of the Commission and to which the States members of the organization have transferred, in whole or in part, competences with regard to the matters covered by this Convention. The accession of such regional economic integration organizations shall be the subject of consultations among Members of the Commission.

Article XXX

1. This Convention may be amended at any time.

2. If one-third of the Members of the Commission request a meeting to discuss a proposed amendment the Depositary shall call such a meeting.

3. An amendment shall enter into force when the Depositary has received instruments of ratification, acceptance or approval thereof from all the Members of the Commission.

4. Such amendment shall thereafter enter into force as to any other Contracting Party when notice of ratification, acceptance or approval by it has been received by the Depositary. Any such Contracting Party from which no such notice has been received within a period of one year from the date of entry into force of the amendment in accordance with paragraph 3 above shall be deemed to have withdrawn from this Convention.

Article XXXI

1. Any Contracting Party may withdraw from this Convention on 30 June of any year, by giving written notice not later than 1 January of the same year to the Depositary, which, upon receipt of such a notice, shall communicate it forthwith to the other Contracting Parties.

2. Any other Contracting Party may, within sixty days of the receipt of a copy of such a notice from the Depositary, give written notice of withdrawal to the Depositary in which case the Convention shall cease to be in force on 30 June of the same year with respect to the Contracting Party giving such notice.

3. Withdrawal from this Convention by any Member of the Commission shall not affect its financial obligations under this Convention.

Article XXXII

The Depositary shall notify all Contracting Parties of the following:

   a. signatures of this Convention and the deposit of instruments of ratification, acceptance, approval or accession;

   b. the date of entry into force of this Convention and of any amendment thereto.

Article XXXIII

1. This Convention, of which the English, French, Russian and Spanish texts are equally authentic, shall be deposited with the Government of Australia which shall transmit duly certified copies thereof to all signatory and acceding Parties.

2. This Convention shall be registered by the Depositary pursuant to Article 102 of the Charter of the United Nations.

Drawn up at Canberra this twentieth day of May 1980.

In Witness Whereof the undersigned, being duly authorized, have signed this Convention.

[*Here follow the signatures on behalf of the parties to the Agreement, including Australia.*]

Annex for an Arbitral Tribunal

1. The arbitral tribunal referred to in paragraph 3 of Article XXV shall be composed of three arbitrators who shall be appointed as follows:

a. The Party commencing proceedings shall communicate the name of an arbitrator to the other Party which, in turn, within a period of forty days following such notification, shall communicate the name of the second arbitrator. The Parties shall, within a period of sixty days following appointment of the second arbitrator, appoint the third arbitrator, who shall not be a national of either Party and shall not be of the same nationality as either of the first two arbitrators. The third arbitrator shall preside over the tribunal.

b. If the second arbitrator has not been appointed within the prescribed period, or if the Parties have not reached agreement within the prescribed period on the appointment of the third arbitrator, that arbitrator shall be appointed, at the request of either Party, by the Secretary-General of the Permanent Court of Arbitration, from among persons of international standing not having the nationality of a State which is a Party to this Convention.

2. The arbitral tribunal shall decide where its headquarters will be located and shall adopt its own rules of procedure.

3. The award of the arbitral tribunal shall be made by a majority of its members, who may not abstain from voting.

4. Any Contracting Party which is not a Party to the dispute may intervene in the proceedings with the consent of the arbitral tribunal.

5. The award of the arbitral tribunal shall be final and binding on all Parties to the dispute and on any Party which intervenes in the proceedings and shall be complied with without delay. The arbitral tribunal shall interpret the award at the request of one of the Parties to the dispute or of any intervening Party.

6. Unless the arbitral tribunal determines otherwise because of the particular circumstances of the case, the expenses of the tribunal, including the remuneration of its members, shall be borne by the Parties to the dispute in equal shares.

Impact of the Law of the Sea Convention

The United Nations Law of the Sea Convention, when completed and brought into force, will put pressure directly on the Antarctic Treaty Parties. It will require all countries to notify the United Nations of the limits of their national jurisdiction. Coastal countries will be required to notify the United Nations' Secretary General of the outer limits of their continental shelves. These requirements will pose a dilemma both for claimants and non-claimants.

Article VI of the Antarctic Treaty provides that while the Treaty applies to the entire area south of 60°S latitude, nothing in it 'shall prejudice or in any way affect the rights, or the exercise of rights, of any State under international law with regard to the high seas within that area'.

The Law of the Sea Convention will establish a new, international legal regime for minerals beyond the limits of national jurisdiction — giving effect to the principle of the *common heritage of mankind*. This raises the important issue in the Antarctic: what areas *are* beyond the limits of 'national jurisdiction'?

The non-claimants' position that territorial claims on the continent are invalid leads to the following conclusion:

i. there are no territorial seas around Antarctic, and

ii. there are no 200-mile (333 kilometre) exclusive economic zones, or continental shelves under the jurisdiction of any nation. See map page 17 for extent of exclusive economic zones (EEZs) if they were declared.

If this is so, the International Seabed Authority might reasonably be seen as having jurisdiction over all marine areas in the region once the new Law of the Sea Convention enters into force. This is vociferously disputed by the claimants.

In discussions recently on this issue, the Consultative Parties have acknowledged the Seabed Authority *will* have a role in the region, but only at that point where the Parties' jurisdiction ends.

There has been no internal agreement whether Antarctic Treaty governments will base their claim to jurisdiction and/or control over marine areas around the continent on the claimants' 'sovereignty' or on some collective 'right' derived under the Treaty.

Policy of Voluntary Restraint by the Treaty Parties

At the eighth Consultative Meeting a resolution about minerals called for all members of the world community to refrain from commercial exploration and exploitation in order to enable the Treaty Parties to seek 'timely agreed solutions'.

In 1977 at the ninth Consultative Meeting, the Parties agreed again to refrain from conducting any commercial exploration and exploitation activities for Antarctic minerals while 'progress' is made on development of a legal regime.

The voluntary restraint policy on minerals activities was reviewed by the Consultative Parties at the 10th and 11th Meetings and remains in force. Recommendation X-1 (1979) provides as follows:

'An agreed regime on Antarctic mineral resources should include *inter alia* means for:

i. assessing the possible impact of mineral resource activities on the Antarctic environment in order to provide for information decision-making;

ii. determining whether mineral resources activities will be acceptable;

iii. governing the ecological, technological, political, legal, and economic aspects of those activities in cases where they would be determined acceptable; including:

a. establishing, as an important part of the regime, rules relating to the protection of the Antarctic environment; and

b. requiring that mineral resource activities undertaken pursuant to the regime be undertaken in compliance with such rules.'

The Consultative Parties have also agreed that, in dealing with the question of Antarctic mineral resources, they should not prejudice the 'interests of all mankind' in Antarctica (Resolution IX-1), although it is not clear exactly what this is intended to accomplish.

Recommendations of Second World Conference on National Parks

The Group recommended to governments that 'high priority be given to the conservation of representative biomes and ecosystems on land and sea that are still virtually undisturbed', and 'in particular . . . that special attention be given to . . . polar regions . . .'

Recommendation 5 called on governments to establish Antarctica as a World Park under the auspices of the United Nations:

'Recognizing the great scientific and aesthetic value of the unaltered natural ecosystems of the Antarctic Continent and the seas surrounding it;

Recognizing that the Antarctic Treaty provides, to an unprecendented degree, protection to these ecosystems;

Believing that, in this second century of the national park movement, the concept of world parks should be promoted;

Considering that Antarctica offers special opportunities for the implementation of this concept;

The Second World Conference on National Parks, meeting at Grand Teton National Park, USA, in September 1972:

Recommends that the nations party to the Antarctic Treaty should negotiate to establish the Antarctic Continent and the surrounding seas as the first world park, under the auspices of the United Nations.'

Biomass

The SCAR Group of Specialists on Southern Ocean Ecosystems and their Living Resources, co-sponsored by the Scientific Committee on Oceanic Research (SCOR), the Advisory Committee of Experts on Marine Resources Research (ACMRR) of the Food and Agriculture Organisation of the United Nations and the International Association of Biological Oceanographers (IABO), continues to refine and develop the ten year international BIOMASS programme.

The BIOMASS programme represents the first co-ordinated international research programme to provide a basis for wise management of the living resources of the Southern Ocean.

The principal scientific focus is on Antarctic krill, the key species in the food web.

SCAR, in preparation for this major, multinational multidisciplinary, co-ordinated research programme, established subgroups to advise on the programme.

SCAR Group of Specialists on Southern Ocean Ecosystems and Their Living Resources (co-sponsored by SCOR, IABO, and ACMRR)

Technical Group (3)
- Programme Implementation and co-ordination
- Methods
- Data, Statistics, and Resource Evaluation

Working Parties (5)
- Acoustic Krill Estimation
- Krill Biology
- Fish Biology
- Physical and Chemical Oceanography
- Bird Ecology

Organizational structure of advisory activities of the programme 'Biological Investigations of Marine Antarctic Systems and Stocks' (BIOMASS).

In preparation for the first International BIOMASS experiment (FIBEX), the Group of Specialists met in Krakow, Poland, September 1979, to lay plans and develop research priorities. Meetings were also held of the Technical Groups on Program Implementation and Co-ordination (Buenos Aires, June 1979); Data, Statistics and Resource Evaluation (Woods Hole, August 1979); and Methods (Buenos Aires, May 1979). BIOMASS Working Parties on Fish Biology, Acoustic Estimation of Krill Abundance, and Bird Biology also met. A *BIOMASS Newsletter*, *BIOMASS Report Series*, and a *BIOMASS Directory* have been issued by SCAR. A Series of BIOMASS method manuals and *BIOMASS, Volume II: Selected Contributions from the Woods Hole Conference on Living Resources of the Southern Ocean* were issued during 1980.

Research vessels from twelve countries participated in FIBEX. A major endeavour of FIBEX was a multiship krill acoustic survey in the western part of the Atlantic sector, with supporting parallel studies in the eastern Atlantic, India and Pacific sectors.

The objective of the survey was to estimate distribution and abundance of krill and to determine feasibility of echo surveys for krill stock assessment.

According to the summary documents for this project, the data includes:

1. acoustic survey of krill abundance in the Western Atlantic sector;
2. accompanying observations of phytoplankton abundance, mixed layer depth, zooplankton samples and observations of birds, seals and whales;
3. patch studies from krill (involving information on morphology, density and temporal variation of swarms), swarm composition by size, sex and maturity stage, and physical, chemical and biological environment interactions;
4. fish population studies.

Accompanying observations were made on phytoplankton abundance and primary production. Medium and small-scale studies of krill swarming behaviour were carried out, and complementary share-based studies and a survey of Antarctic seabirds were also done.

Data from FIBEX were reviewed at a conference in Hamburg, Federal Republic of Germany, in October 1981. *The most critical problems for BIOMASS continue to be:*

1. lack of a centralized computer data facility; and
2. research funds. In general, research money to determine location and size of krill swarms has been easier to obtain than funds for ecosystem research.

A second International BIOMASS Experiment (SIBEX) is planned for 1982-84.

International Union for Conservation of Nature and Natural Resources — 1981 General Assembly Resolution

ANTARCTICA ENVIRONMENT AND THE SOUTHERN OCEAN

Preamble

1. *Recognizing* the importance of Antarctica and its Continental shelf ('the Antarctic environment') and the Southern Ocean for the world as a whole, particularly in maintaining the stability of the global marine environment and atmosphere, and the paramount importance to mankind of its great wilderness qualities (for science, education and inspiration);

2. *Recalling* the continued and long established interest that IUCN has in the conservation of the ecosystems of the Antarctica environment as well as in the conservation of the species and habitats that it supports;

3. *Mindful* that the World Conservation Strategy (prepared by IUCN with the advice, cooperation and financial assistance of UNEP and WWF and in collaboration with FAO and UNESCO) identifies Antarctica and the Southern Ocean as a priority for international action;

4. *Noting* that eleven Antarctic Treaty Consultative Parties are represented in IUCN and that they have already espoused the aims of the World Conservation Strategy;

5. *Aware* of the achievements of the Consultative Parties in their stewardship under the Antarctic Treaty in protecting the Antarctica environment from harmful interference, and the provision of measures for the conservation of flora and fauna, guidelines to minimize harmful effects of human activities, and measures specifically related to tourism activities;

6. *Also Cognizant* of the fact that the Consultative Parties are presently considering the establishment of a regime to govern both commercial exploration and exploitation of any mineral resources should this ever prove acceptable and that any exploitation of minerals would adversely affect the values of the Antarctica environment;

7. *Further Aware* of the additional efforts of the same nations to enhance the conservation and sustainable use of the living resources of the region, in particular by the initiative taken to negotiate and adopt the Convention for the Conservation of Antarctic Seals (1972) and the Convention on the Conservation of Antarctic Marine Living Resources (1980);

8. *Taking Note* of the action taken by the International Whaling Commission with regard to whaling in the Southern Ocean and the relevance to that ocean of other activities affecting conservation of the marine environment generally;

9. *Recalling* that the Second World Conference on National Parks in 1972 recommended that nations party to the Antarctic Treaty should establish the Antarctic Continent and surrounding seas as the first World Park and that other protective designations are being proposed to reflect the unique status of the area;

10. *Concerned* further that the effective planning, management and conservation of the Antarctica environment can only be achieved by thorough consideration of feasible alternatives and if all actions are based on restraint and scientific knowledge, as well as through cooperation and coordination;

The General Assembly of IUCN, at its 15th Session in Christchurch, New Zealand, 11-23 October 1981:

THE ANTARCTICA ENVIRONMENT

General

11. *Strongly Recommends* that the Antarctic Treaty Consultative Parties should further enhance the status of the Antarctica environment and foster measures which would:

   a. maintain for all time the intrinsic values of the Antarctica environment for mankind and the global ecosystem;

   b. ensure that all human activities are compatible with the maintenance of these values;

   c. ascribe to the Antarctica environment as a whole a designation which connotes worldwide its unique character and values and the special measures accorded to its planning, management and conservation;

12. *Urges* the Parties to ensure the protection of the Antarctica environment from harmful interference, as expressed in Recommendation 5 of the Ninth Meeting of the Consultative Parties;

MINERALS

13. *Urges* that no mineral regime be brought into operation until such time as full consideration has been given to protecting the Antarctica environment completely from minerals activities and the environmental risks have been fully ascertained and safeguards developed to avoid adverse environmental effects;

Communication and Consultation

14. *Urges* the Consultative Parties to recognize the increased interest in the Antarctica environment of the world community, and therefore that they:

   a. mobilise and draw upon the goodwill and expertise freely available to support their work by effective communication and consultation with interested parties;

b. foster public interest and awareness by well-informed educative measures based on accurate reporting and dissemination of their policies and actions in relation to the Antarctica environment; and

c. invite representatives from appropriate non-governmental organisations (including IUCN and ASOC) to participate in meetings according to normal international practice;

15. *Further Urges* national delegations to the Antarctic Treaty to keep fully in touch and consult with NGOs in their countries concerned with the Antarctica environment and to include advisers from these bodies in their delegations;

Membership

16. *Urges* all nations concerned with the future of the Antarctica environment to accede to the Antarctic Treaty;

Research and Conservation — General

17. *Considers* that the Antarctic Treaty Consultative Parties should ensure that research and conservation action is coordinated and that, as a priority, the research programmes needed to protect the Antarctic ecosystem and allow informed decision-making are ascertained, together with the institutions best suited to undertake them;

18. *Urges* full support to on-going scientific efforts and the undertaking of long term, large scale cooperative research programmes focused on the ecological structure and processes of the Antarctica environment and on their role with regard to globally relevant phenomena, such as weather and climate;

19. *Stresses* the necessity to possess sufficient results of such research before management decisions are taken with regard to both living and non-living resources and the need to maintain this research effort so that such decisions may be related to a continuously evolving situation;

20. *Calls Upon* the Consultative Parties to take the lead in such research and conservation programmes;

21. *Urges* all organizations whose activities and expertise are of relevance to these research and conservation tasks to contribute as appropriate;

22. *Pledges* the support and expertise of IUCN in the establishment and carrying out of such programmes;

23. **And Particularly Recommends that:**

a. the Consultative Parties expand the network of sites meriting special protection within the overall framework of measures for the Antarctica environment;

b. continued attention be given to coordination of research and other activities now being carried out in Antarctica to prevent or minimize harmful environmental consequences such as air pollution and wastes;

c. continuous monitoring be made of the consequences of tourism activities, applying strict controls as necessary;

d. the possible ecological impact of the utilization of icebergs be studied and ascertained well in advance of any such utilization;

e. vigilance be exercised on the implementation of the measures prohibiting the introduction of alien species.

The Convention on the Conservation of Antarctic Marine Living Resources 1980

25. *Expresses* its satisfaction that the Marine Living Resources Convention provides the elements necessary to realise an ecosystem approach to the conservation and management of the natural resources of the area;

26. *Pledges* to make IUCN expertise available to the Commission and the Scientific Committee created under the Convention and urges the development of cooperative relationships with the Commission and Scientific Committee, as foreseen by Article XXIII of the Convention;

27. *Recalls* that the dynamics of the Southern Ocean are still poorly known, and urges the Parties to the Convention to exercise caution in its implementation by:

a. developing all fisheries only in conjunction with scientific advice designed to provide the best understanding of the functioning of the ecosystem, and, as a consequence;

b. establishing all such fisheries on an experimental basis for an adequate length of time, with an initial conservative quota by area and appropriate enforcement of such quotas.

28. *Urges* further that:

a. as a high priority feeding grounds of threatened and endangered whales be identified and closed to krill fishing;

b. some areas be closed to fishing *ab initio*, and at least one large sanctuary be established where krill harvesting would be prohibited or permitted only for scientific purposes, in order to provide for adequate baseline areas;

c. an evaluation be made of the role and status of finfish and squid before substantial exploitation takes place;

d. all data be provided, on an agreed standardized scientific basis, including that from fishing operations carried out over a reasonable past period of time, to facilitate the establishment of a central data bank which can utilise data from all relevant sources;

e. appropriate coordination of objectives and activities under the International Whaling Commission be established, in particular over the implementation of measures aiming at the recovery of those whales whose populations have been depleted;

f. the development of dynamic models of the Southern Ocean ecosystem be initiated, bearing in mind the depletion of many whale species;

g. in the process of developing the fishery on a scientific basis, the development of cooperative relationships with appropriate organizations be effectively carried out.

29. *Recommends* further that the Parties to the Convention better inform the scientific and conservation communities of the action they take to protect the Southern Ocean, including reporting on discussions and actions pertaining to environmental conservation issues, and inviting representatives from appropriate NGOs (such as IUCN and ASOC) to participate in appropriate meetings;

30. *Urges* that IUCN be given accredited status as an adviser to the Scientific Committee of the Convention Commission;

31. *Urges* all nations concerned with the future of the Antarctica environment and the Southern Ocean to support the operation of the Convention and to accede to it as soon as possible;

32. *Recommends* that, notwithstanding current worldwide economic difficulties, the significance of the Southern Ocean demands that it be accorded high priority in the allocation of resources adequate to ensure the effective operation of the Commission and its Scientific Committee.

The Minerals of Antarctica

33. *Commends* the Consultative Parties for their decision to refrain from exploration of Antarctic mineral resources for the time being;

34. *Urges* that the Treaty Parties keep IUCN and the scientific and conservation communities well informed of any proposed activities in the Antarctica environment and *urges* further that they seek the views of IUCN on any which would affect the conservation of the Antarctica environment;

35. *Pledges* to make IUCN expertise available to the Treaty Parties and other bodies and organizations as appropriate to conduct or cooperate in conducting studies necessary to ensure that activities carried on in Antarctica have minimum effects on the ecosystem considered.

This 15th General Assembly, in Consequence, Instructs
Council, the Commissions, and the Director General of IUCN

A. to take all steps necessary in the implementation of the pledges which it has made in relation to the Antarctica environment and the Southern Ocean and, in particular, to ensure that, wherever possible, IUCN representation at relevant meetings related thereto is by persons with appropriate expertness;

B. so soon as financial resources permit, to ensure that IUCN's Programme during the coming triennium has regard to the necessity of monitoring developments pertinent to the conservation of species and habitats of Antarctica and the Southern Ocean, and of the ecosystems of which they are a part, with a view to making appropriate recommendations to governments during the coming triennium;

C. to initiate the preparation of a Conservation Strategy for the Antarctica environment and the Southern Ocean in cooperation with the world scientific and conservation communities and to foster appropriate scientific and educational programmes, collaborating on these, where relevant, with the Scientific Committee of the Commission on Marine Living Resources;

D. in particular in this Strategy, to seek appropriate forms of designation for the Antarctica environment as a whole and the specific sites within it which merit special attention;

E. to seek the necessary additional resources for this ANTARCTICA PROJECT.

Resolution of Non Government Organizations Concerning Antarctica and the Southern Ocean

RECOGNIZING the importance of Antarctica and its Continental shelf ('the Antarctica environment') and the Southern Ocean for the world as a whole, particularly in maintaining the stability of the global marine environment and atmosphere, and the paramount importance to mankind of its great wilderness qualities (for science, education and inspiration);

MINDFUL that the World Conservation Strategy (prepared by IUCN with the advice, co-operation and financial assistance of UNEP and WWF and in collaboration with FAO and UNESCO) identifies Antarctica and the Southern Ocean as a priority for international action;

NOTING that elevant Antarctic Treaty Consultative Parties are represented in IUCN and that they have already espoused the aims of the World Conservation Strategy;

AWARE of the achievements of the Consultative Parties in their stewardship under the Antarctic Treaty in protecting the Antarctica environment from harmful interference, and the provision of measures for the conservation of flora and fauna, guidelines to minimize harmful effects of human activities, and measures specifically related to tourism activities;

CONCERNED further that the Antarctic Treaty expires in 1992 and that the effective planning, management and conservation of the Antarctica environment and the equitable and sustained use of its resources can only be achieved by a thorough consideration by all nations of all feasible alternatives, and only if actions are based on scientific knowledge and sound environment principles as well as through co-operation and co-ordination;

THAT this Session of Special Character of the United Nations Environment Programme in Nairobi, Kenya, 10-18 May, 1982:

CALLS UPON the Antarctic Treaty Consultative Parties to open its forums at both the Convention on Antarctic Marine Living Resources Commission and Minerals Regime meetings to all nations and to Non-Governmental Organizations, including the Antarctic and Southern Ocean Coalition, enabling a wider international participation in the decisions affecting Antarctica's future.

URGES the United Nations to take particular note of the present developments affecting Antarctica's future and to use every available opportunity to elevate its importance at all appropriate international forums;

STRONGLY RECOMMENDS to the General Assembly that support and funds should be made available for the convening of a special conference on Antarctica before 1985 that would assess environmental impacts upon the Antarctic ecosystem and review the financial, technological and institutional measures which would have to be undertaken to properly manage the Antarctic ecosystem in the interests of all nations; and

REQUESTS the Antarctic Treaty powers and the United Nations General Assembly to give serious consideration to declaring Antarctica a World Park, in recognition of its inestimable value to humankind, and its status as a global commons.

World Conservation Strategy
—— Objectives for Antarctica

This document was prepared by IUCN, World Wildlife Fund and UNEP in 1980.

Section 18 contains goals for Antarctica:

'Any regime for the exploitation of the living marine resources of the Southern Ocean should so regulate the krill fishery as to prevent:

1. Irreversible changes in the population of krill.

2. Irreversible changes in the population of *Baleen Whales* and those seal, fish and bird species which feed on krill, as well as in the Southern Ocean ecosystem as a whole.

3. Over-capitalisation of krill fishing fleets, which could make it more difficult to agree on a reduction of the krill take should this prove necessary, and could have severe impacts on fisheries outside the Southern Ocean, due to the need to redeploy the krill fleets during the Artarctic winter. An independent observer system be provided for in these regulations.'

The Antarctic Treaty powers and nations fishing should exercise extreme restraint on catch levels until understanding of this uniquely productive ecosystem improves.

All harvesting should be on experimental basis as part of a scientific research programme to improve knowledge of krill and of the Southern Ocean as a whole. Baseline areas where no krill or other living or non-living resources may be taken should be set aside and given complete protection, so that impacts outside can be monitored and evaluated correctly.

Current research efforts should be strongly supported; and the collective analysis and dissemination of biological information should be mandatory. An International Decade of Southern Ocean Research, focusing particularly on ecological processes should be initiated as a matter of urgency.

Investigations of the possible environmental impacts of tourism, scientific research, mining and oil exploitation should be continued. Since oil degrades extremely slowly in conditions such as those of Antarctica and since operating hazards are very high, the feasibility of oil exploration and exploitation should be approached with the utmost caution.

Acronyms

ACMRR: Advisory Committee on Marine Resources Research of FAO.

ASOC: Antarctic and Southern Ocean Coalition.

BIOMASS: Biological Investigations of Marine Species and Stocks.

FAO: Food and Agriculture Organization of the United Nations.

FIBEX: First International BIOMASS Experiment.

GARP: Global Atmospheric Research Programme.

IABO: International Association for Biological Oceanography.

ICES: International Council for the Exploration of the Sea.

ICSU: International Council of Scientific Unions.

IIED: International Institute for Environment and Development.

IOC: Intergovernmental Oceanographic Commission.

ISOS: International Southern Ocean Studies.

IUCN: International Union for the Conservation of Nature and Natural Resources.

IWC: International Whaling Commission.

SCAR: Scientific Committee on Antarctic Research.

SCOR: Scientific Committee on Oceanic Research.

SOC: Southern Ocean Co-ordination Group.

UNDP: United Nations Development Programme.

UNEP: United Nations Environment Programme.

UNESCO: United Nations Education, Scientific and Cultural Organization.

WCS: World Conservation Strategy.

WWF: World Wildlife Fund.

WMO: World Meterological Organization.

Auburn, F. A., Antarctic Law & Politics, Indianna University Press, 1982.

Barnes, J. N., The Emerging Antarctic Marine Living Resources Convention: Meeting the New Realities of Resource Exploitation in the Southern Ocean, Center for Law and Social Policy, Washington, D.C.

—— 'Last Chance for Wild Antarctica', in The Living Wilderness, June 1979.

Barnes, J. N., Jackson, T., and Rich, B., Introduction to Southern Ocean Issues, Oceanic Society, 1980.

Beddington, J. R., Modelling and Management of the Southern Ocean, Report to IUCN, 1979.

Bengston, J. L., Review of Information Regarding the Conservation of the Antarctic Marine Ecosystem, Marine Mammal Commission Report, 1978.

Bertrand, K. J., Americans in Antarctica 1775-1948, American Geographical Society, 1971.

Brewster, B., Antarctica: Wilderness at Risk, Friends of the Earth, 1982.

Brown, L. R., The Twenty-Ninth Day, W. W. Norton & Co, 1978.

Chapman, W. (ed.), Antarctic Conquest: The Great Explorers in Their Own Words, Bobbs Merrill, 1965.

Charney, J. (ed.), The New Nationalism and the Use of Common Spaces: Issues in Marine Pollution and the Exploitation of Antarctica, Osmun, 1982.

Central Intelligence Agency, Polar Regions Atlas, 1978.

Everson, I., The Living Resources of the Southern Ocean, FAO, Rome, 1977.

Green, K., Role of Krill in the Antarctic Marine Ecosystem, in Final Environmental Impact Statement on the Negotiation of a Regime for Conservation of Antarctic Marine Living Resources, Appendix E, US Department of State, 1978.

Halle, L. J., The Sea and the Ice, Houghton Mifflin, Boston, 1973.

Hofman, R. J., Conservation of Living Resources in Antarctica, Transaction of the 44th North American Wildlife and Natural Resources Conference, Wildlife Management Institute, Washington, D.C., 1979.

Holdgate, M. W. (ed.), Antarctic Ecology, 1970.

Holdgate, M. and Tinker, J., Oil and Other Minerals in Antarctica, Bellagio Report, SCAR, 1979.

Holt, S. J. & Talbot, L. M., New Principles for the Conservation of Wild Living Resources, The Wildlife Society, 1978.

Institute of Polar Studies, A Framework for Assessing Environmental Impacts of Possible Antarctic Mineral Development, Ohio State University, 1977.

International Council for the Exploration of the Sea Report of the Ad Hoc Meeting on the Provision of Advice on the Biological Basis for Fisheries Management. Cooperative Research Report 62, Charlottenland, 1976.

King, H. C. R., The Antarctic, Arco, New York, 1969.

Langone, J., Life at the Bottom: the People of Antarctica, Little, Brown, Boston, 1977.

Larkin, P. A., An Epitaph for the Concept of Maximum Sustainable Yields, Transactions Am. Fish Soc. 1977.

Lavign, D. M., Management of Seals in the North-West Atlantic Ocean, Transactions of the 44th American Wildlife and Natural Resources Conference, Wildlife Management Institute, Washington, D.C., 1979.

Laws, R. T., Seals and Whales in Southern Ocean, Phil. Transactions of Royal Society, Donlocdon Bulletin, 279:81-96, 1977.

Lewis, R. S., A Continent for Science, Viking Press, New York, 1965.

Lewis, R. S. & Smith, P. M. (ed.), Frozen Future: A Prophetic Report from Antarctica, Quadrangle Books, 1973.

Mawson, D., The Home of the Blizzard, Lippincott, Philadelphia, 1914.

May, R., Beddington, J., Clark, W. W., Holt, S. J., Laws, R. M., Management of Multispecies Fisheries, Science, Vol. 205, 1979.

McWhinnie, M. A. (ed.), Polar Research: To the Present, and the Future, AAAS, Washington, 1978.

Mitchell, B. and Kimball, L., Conflict Over the Cold Continent, 35 For. Pol. 124, 1979.

Mitchell, B. & Sandbrook, R., Antarctica and Its Resources, Earthscan (IIED), London, 1980.

—— The Management of the Southern Ocean, London, 1980.

Neider, C. (ed.), Antarctica: Authentic Accounts of Life and Exploration, Random House, New York, 1972.

—— Edge of the World: Ross Island, Antarctica, Doubleday, 1974.

Parker, B., (ed.), Environmental Impact in Antarctica, 1978.

Payne, I., Crisis on World Fisheries, New Scientist, 26 May 1977.

Peterson, R. J., Penguins, Houghton, Mifflin, 1979.

Porter, E., Antarctica, E. P. Dutton, 1978.

Quam, L. (ed.), Research in the Antarctic, AAAS, Washington, 1971.

SCAR/SCOR Group of Specialists on Living Resources of the Southern Ocean, Biological Investigations of Marine Antarctic Systems and Stocks, BIOMASS, 1977.

—— Meeting, Kiel, Federal Republic of Germany, 30 May-2 June 1978. Final Report. BIOMASS Report Series 1.

—— Technical Groups on Data, Statistics and Resource Evaluation, Report of First Meeting, BIOMASS Report Series 4.

—— Technical Group on Program Implementation and Coordination of FIBEX, Buenos Aires, Argentina, 6-8 June 1979. Report of the First Meeting. BIOMASS Report Series 6 (cited as FIBEX implementation report).

—— Meeting, Krakow, Poland, September 1979. BIOMASS Report, Series 7.

Sullivan, W., Quest for a Continent, McGraw Hill, 1957.

Suter, Dr K. D., World Law and the Lost Wilderness, Friends of the Earth and Second Back Row Press, Sydney, 1979.

Twiss, J. R., Research Needed to Assure Conservation of Southern Ocean Resources, prepared for Marine Mammal Commission, 1978 (unpublished).

Zumberge, J. H. (ed,), Possible Environmental Effects of Mineral Exploration and Exploitation in Antarctica, EAMREA Report, SCAR, 1979.

Glossary

Acoustic survey: use of sound waves (sonar) transmitted and reflected to detect and locate underwater objects; such echo surveys are the most practical means of surveying krill and fish individuals and swarms.

Amphipods: any of numerous small crustaceans of the order Amphipoda.

Antarctic Convergence: the natural oceanic and biological boundary of the Southern Ocean. Lying between 47° and 64°S, it is the place where cold Antarctic waters sink beneath warmer waters moving south resulting in an abrupt surface temperature change of as much as 7°F (4°C). It is also the outer boundary of the area covered by the Antarctic Marine Living Resources Convention.

Baleen whales: whales which lack teeth and which filter their food through a beleen or whalebone which consists of elastic, hornlike material forming plates in the upper jaw. There are five principle species of Baleen whales in the Southern Ocean: Blue, Humpback, Fin, Sei and Minke.

Benthos, Benthic: referring to the bottom of the sea, or the organisms which live on the sea bottom.

Biomass: the amount of living matter in the form of one or more kinds of organisms present in a particular habitat, usually expressed as weight of organisms per unit area of habitat or as volume or weight of organisms per unit volume of habitat.

Catastrophe: abrupt, discontinuous, irreversible change in a system; recent mathematical theory has developed general models for various prototypal catastrophes; changes in various natural systems, including ecosystems, can be analysed in terms of these models.

Cephalopod: any of various mollusks (marine invertebrates) of the class Cephalopoda, such as an octopus or squid, having a beaked head, an internal shell in some species, and prehensile tentacles.

Copepods: any of numerous small marine and freshwater crustaceans of the order Copepoda; copepods are potential competitors for the ecological niche of krill in the Southern Ocean.

Euphausiids: an order of small, commonly lumenescent crustaceans resembling shrimps, forming in some areas an important element of marine plankton.

Fin fish: a 'true' fish, as distinguished from a shell fish.

Herbivore: a plant-eating animal or fish.

Hydrography: the scientific description and analysis of the physical conditions, boundaries, flow and related characteristics of oceans and other surface waters.

Incidental catch: in fishing, the accidental or incidental catch of non-target species; the incidental catch of dolphins in tuna fishing is an example.

Krill: small marine crustaceans of the order Euphausiacea, constituting the principle food of baleen whales.

Maximum Sustainable Yield (MSY): exploitation of a single species, viewed apart from all other elements in the ecosystem, so that the maximum yield is obtained while maintaining the population level of the exploited species which gives this yield; for most fish MSY is obtained when the exploited populations is at 40 to 60 per cent of its pristine level. See Sustainable Yield.

Phytoplankton: minute, floating aquatic plants.

Plankton: passably floating or weakly swimming animal and plant life of a body of water consisting chiefly of minute plants and animals.

Recruitment: increment to a natural population.

Swarming: refers to the behaviour of krill and many species of fish which aggregate in large, dense schools or swarms.

Sustainable yield: the harvesting level of a given population level of a species — be it 10 per cent or 100 per cent of the population's pristine level — which will maintain the population at that level.

Trophic ladder: the hierarchy of organisms in an ecosystem according to the level of their food consumption; the food web: an organism which feeds on another is one step higher on the trophic ladder.

Trophodynamics: the dynamics, processes, and relations of organisms on the trophic ladder; e.g., which organisms feed upon which other organisms and how and when.

Zooplankton: animal life of the plankton.

Organizations Interested in Antarctica

1 International Union for the Conservation of Nature and Natural Resources (IUCN) and the World Wildlife Fund (WWF)

IUCN is an independent, international, non-government organization.[1] It was established in 1948 to promote the protection and sustainable use of living natural resources, based on scientific principles and adequate research.

IUCN's global network, in addition to the membership, comprises over 3000 scientists and other experts in all phases of conservation, participating in the work of IUCN commissions and centres.

From its inception in September 1961, WWF has worked to support wildlife and wild habitats. It raises money for a wide range of conservation programmes around the world, in conjunction with IUCN.

IUCN and WWF were actively involved in the preparatory work for the Convention on the Conservation of Antarctic Marine Living Resources. IUCN and WWF carried out two joint projects with the International Institute for Environment and Development (IIED) on 'Living Resources Management of Southern Ocean Ecosystems', and on 'Krill and Southern Ocean Management Options'. They co-sponsored a 1980 Washington workshop of scientific experts on krill fishing around Antarctica with the Center for Law and Social Policy and the Oceanic Society.

Another joint project with IIED aims at improving the scientific basis for sustainable utilization of krill, through a series of case studies concentrating particularly on krill and whale interactions. Dr John Beddington has been directing this study.

IUCN has set out objectives for protecting Antarctica in the World Conservation Strategy defining long range conservation goals for this part of the global commons.

At its 1981 General Assembly, IUCN passed a resolution on Antarctica calling for protection and understanding of the Antarctic region. It is contained in Appendix I.

2 International Whaling Commission (IWC)

Because the IWC has protected all whale stocks in the Southern Ocean except for minke whales, it will have an important role to play in helping to implement the 'ecosystem' approach of the Marine Living Resources Convention.

[1] IUCN has 480 member groups in 100 countries, including 56 sovereign states, 116 government agencies and over 300 non-government organizations.

The new Convention explicitly acknowledges the need for consultation with the IWC. The IWC was invited to send an observer to the May 1980 conference which concluded the Convention and to the preparatory meeting held in Hobart in September 1981.

The IWC Scientific Committee is in possession of large quantities of data pertinent to the 'ecosystem' regime. But there is no agreement yet on a centralized computer data centre, or a commitment of the formal resources necessary to operate such a centre.

The IWC is important because of its relatively enlightened practices of attendance and participation at meetings by non-government observers, its rules on publication of data, rights and procedure. These issues are of real concern to conservation and environmental organizations in the context of the Antarctic Marine Living Resources Convention.

3 Scientific Committee for Antarctic Research (SCAR)

SCAR is a non-governmental organization created as a committee of the International Council of Scientific Unions. Scientists from twenty-three countries presently participate in its work, helping to co-ordinate scientific activity in Antarctica.

SCAR membership parallels that of the voting members to the Antarctic Treaty. Its meetings are informal. Recommendations and resolutions are advisory only and not binding on member governments and scientific organizations. SCAR's work is not constrained by the unanimity or consensus requirement.

SCAR usually addresses most scientific issues before they are considered in depth at Antarctic Treaty Consultative meetings. SCAR has taken a number of important initiatives in Antarctica. Its proposals for conserving Antarctic seal stocks were put to a special conference of Parties to the Antarctic Treaty in 1972 and resulted in the conclusion that year of the Convention for the Conservation of Antarctic Seals.

Recently SCAR launched a ten year co-ordinated international research programme for the Biological Investigations of Marine Antarctic Systems and Stocks (BIOMASS).

One problem SCAR has faced repeatedly has been the failure of governments to provide financial resources necessary to carry out its important tasks. This has become more acute in recent years as resource issues have emerged.

For example, the task of developing a research programme to implement the ecosystem conservation standard in the new Marine Living Resources Convention is very large and no money has been provided by governments to carry it out.

Governments generally have been unwilling to pay the costs of the large-scale research programme recommended by SCAR, so the BIOMASS programme has not been fully implemented. Governments have not agreed to provide funds for a centralized BIOMASS data centre.

Like all non-government organizations, SCAR is denied access to the decision making process of the Treaty. SCAR representatives are not invited to Consultative meetings.

SCAR was invited to send an observer to the May 1980 meeting which concluded the Antarctic Marine Living Resources Convention and to the preparatory meeting for that Convention held in Hobart, September 1981.

4 Scientific Committee on Oceanic Research (SCOR)

SCOR is one of the sponsors of the BIOMASS programme. SCOR Working Group 54 is also the SCAR Group of Specialists on Southern Ocean Ecosystems.

SCOR was invited to send an observer to the May 1980 meeting which concluded the Antarctic Marine Living Resources Convention and to the preparatory meeting for that Convention held in Hobart, September 1981.

5 Food and Agriculture Organization (FAO)

The Advisory Committee of Experts on Marine Resources Research (ACMRR) of FAO is one of the co-sponsors of the BIOMASS programme. Because of its wide experience with fisheries data, FAO was invited to send an observer to the May 1980 meeting which concluded the Antarctic Marine Living Resources Convention and to the preparatory meeting in Hobart, September 1981.

6 Convention on International Trade in Endangered Species of Wild Fauna and Flora (CITES)

Representatives from CITES should be invited to participate in Antarctic resource meetings. CITES could have a role to play in helping develop the 'ecosystem' approach in the Southern Ocean as several species of whales in the region are listed as threatened or endangered.

CITES employs enlightened practices regarding participation by observers at meetings, and in enforcement of its provisions, offering good models for application to the Antarctic.

ASOC Member Organizations

American Cetacean Society,
PO Box 4416,
San Pedro, California 90731,
USA

American Littoral Society,
Sandy Hook,
Highlands, New Jersey 07732,
USA

Animal Liberation,
18 Argyle Street,
The Rocks, Sydney 2000,
Australia

Animal Societies Federation of NSW,
Suite 9, 17th level,
225 Pitt Street, Sydney 2000,
Australia

Animal Welfare Institute,
PO Box 3650,
Washington, DC, 20007,
USA

ASPCA,
441 East 92nd Street,
New York, New York 10028,
USA

Australian Conservation Foundation,
672B Glenferrie Road,
Hawthorn, Vic 3122
Australia

Australian National Parks Council,
104 Buston Street,
Deakin, ACT 2600,
Australia

Bond Beter Leefmilieu,
Vlaanderen ZVW,
Aarlenstraat 25,
1040 Brussels,
Belgium

Canadian Nature Federation,
75 Albert Street,
Ottawa, KIP 6GI, Ontario
Canada

Centre for Action on Endangered
  Species,
175 West Main Stret,
Ayer, Massachussetts, 01432,
USA

Center for Ocean Studies,
Gardner's Basin,
Atlantic City, New Jersey, 08401,
USA

Centro Cientifico Tropical,
Apartado, 8-3870,
San Jose, Costa Rica,
Central America

An Taisce,
41 Percy Lane,
Dublin 4,
Ireland

Connecticut Cetacean Society,
190 Stilwold Drive,
Weathersfield, Connecticut 06109,
USA

Conservation Council of Victoria,
324 William Street,
Melbourne, Vic 3000,
Australia

Conservation Council of South
  Australia, Inc.,
GPO Box 2403,
Adelaide, SA 5001,
Australia

Defenders of Wildlife,
1244 19th Street, NW,
Washington, DC 20036,
USA

Deutch Naturschutzring,
Alterscheinerstrasse, 20,
8 Munchen 90,
Federal Republic of Germany

Environment and Conservation
  Organizations of New Zealand,
  Inc.,
PO Box 11057,
Wellington 1,
New Zealand

Environmental Defense Fund,
Park Avenue,
New York, New York 10016,
USA

Environmental Defense Fund,
1525 18th Street, NW,
Washington, DC 2009,
USA

Fauna Preservation Society,
c/- London Zoo,
Regents Park, London NW1,
England

Federacion Mesoamericana de
  Asocianciones Conservacion-Istos,
  No Gubernamentales
Apartado 3089,
San Jose, Costa Rica,
Central America

Flemish Youth Federation for the
  Study of Nature and for
  Environmental Conservation,
'Nature 2000' VZW,
c/- Bervoetstratte 33,
B-2000 Antwerpen,
Belgium

Friends of the Earth,
366 Smith Street,
Collingwood, Vic 3066,
Australia

Friends of the Earth,
Roubieszekgasse 2/23,
1100 Wien,
Austria

Friends of the Earth,
5353 Queen Street,
Ottawa, Ontario KIP 5C5,
Canada

Amigos de la Naturaleza,
Apartado 162 Guadalupe,
Costa Rica,
Central America

Friends of the Earth,
9 Poland Street,
London WIV 3DG,
United Kingdom

Chikyu-No-Tomo
(Friends of the Earth),
1-51-8 Yoyogi Shibuya-Ku,
Tokyo 151,
Japan

Freunde der Erde Berlin,
Mehringhof,
Gneisenaustrasse 2,
1000 Berlin 61,
Federal German Republic

Friends of the Earth,
Sahabat Alam Malaysia,
7 Cantonment Road,
Penang,
Malaysia

Friends of the Earth,
Apartado Postal 269,
Cuernavaco, Morelos,
Mexico

Friends of the Earth Ltd.,
PO Box 39-065,
Auckland West,
New Zealand

Friends of the Earth International,
124 Separ Street,
San Francisco, California 94105,
USA

Friends of the Earth,
2A Ainslie Place,
Edinburgh 3,
Scotland

Amigos de la Terre,
Humberto de la Terre,
Campomanes,
13-2⁰ IZQOA, Madrid,
Spain

Friends of the Earth,
PO Box A474,
Sydney South, NSW 2000,
Australia

Friends of the Earth,
530 7th Street, S.E.,
Washington, DC 20003,
USA

Friends of Whales,
10830 SW 85th Court,
Gainesville, Florida 32601,
USA

Friends of Wildlife,
814 W. Markland Drive,
Monterey Park, California 91754,
USA

Forum International,
2437 Durant Avenue #208,
Berkeley, California,
USA

Fund for Animals,
140 West 57th Street,
New York, New York 10019,
USA

Fund for Animals,
1765 P Street, NW,
Washington, DC 20036,
USA

Friends of the Earth,
Witzlebenstrasse 32,
1-Berlin 19,
West Germany

Fund for Animals Ltd.,
PO Box 371,
Manly, NSW 2095,
Australia

Geelong Environment Council,
Box 693,
Geelong, Vic 3220,
Australia

Greenpeace Adelaide,
310 Angus Street,
Adelaide, SA 5000,
Australia

Greenpeace Australia,
399 Pitt Street,
Sydney, NSW 2000,
Australia

Greenpeace Canada,
2623 West 4th Avenue,
Vancouver, BC N5N IK5,
Canada

Greenpeace Denmark,
PO Box 2058,
8240 Reeskof,
Denmark

Greenpeace United Kingdom,
Globe House,
2a Crucifix Lane,
London, SR1,
England

Greenpeace France,
Remi Parmentier,
3 Rue de la Bucherie,
Paris 75005,
France

Greenpeace Germany,
Hohebrucke 1,
Haus der seefahrt,
2000 Hamburg 11,
Federal German Republic

Greenpeace Japan,
Daini Kopo 402,
5-2416 Nakano,
Nakano-ku,
Tokyo,
Japan

Greenpeace Netherlands,
98 Damrak,
1012 1P,
Amsterdam,
Netherlands

Greenpeace New Zealand,
Private Bag,
Wellesley Street,
Auckland,
New Zealand

Greenpeace USA,
240 Fort Mason, BldgE,
San Francisco, California 94123,
USA

Greenpeace,
2007 R Street, NW,
Washington, DC 20009,
USA

Institito de Ecolocia de Chile,
Agustinas N°641-Of,11,
Santiago,
Chile

Institute for Delphinid Research,
Box 694,
Georgetown,
Cayman Islands

International Ecology Society,
1471 Barclay Street,
St Paul, Minnesotta 55106,
USA

International Primate Protection
   League,
PO Drawer X,
Summerville, Sc 29483,
USA

International Fund for Animal
   Welfare,
Box 142,
Elsah, Illinois 62028,
USA

International Fund for Animal
   Welfare,
Private Bag 1, PO,
Bondi Junction, NSW 2024
Australia

International Fund for Animal
   Welfare,
PO Box 193,
Yarmouth Port, Massachusetts 02675,
USA

Irish Wildbird Conservation,
c/- Royal Irish Academy,
19 Dawson Street,
Dublin,
Ireland

Launceston Environmental Centre,
103 Wellington Street,
Launceston, Tas 7250,
Australia

Let Live,
19102 Roman Way,
Gaithersburg, MD 20760,
· USA

Ligue Belge pour la Protection des
   Oiseaux,
9 Durentijdlei B2130,
Brassachat,
Belgium

Marine Action Centre,
9 Whistler Street,
Manly, NSW 2095,
Australia

Marine Action Centre,
The Bathouse,
Gyndin Street,
Cambridge,
England

Monitor International,
19102 Roman Way,
Gaithersburg, MD 20760,
USA

Nacional pro Defensa de la Fauna y
   Flora,
1 Codoiredo Stutzin,
Casille 3075, Santiago,
Chile

National Coalition for Marine
   Conservation,
18th Floor,
100 Federal Street,
Boston, Massachusetts 02110,
USA

National Audubon Society,
950 Third Avenue,
New York, New York 10022,
USA

Natura,
6, Bd F.D. Roosevelt,
L-2450 Luxembourg,
P.P. 91/L,
2010 Luxembourg

Natural Resources Defense Council,
1725 I Street, NW,
Washington, DC 20006,
USA

Nature Conservation Council of NSW,
399 Pitt Street,
Sydney, NSW 2000,
Australia

Ocean Trust Foundation,
312 Sutter Street,
San Francisco, California 94108,
USA

Wildlande and Watershed Project-
   CATIE,
Turrialba,
Costa Rica,
Central America

Project Jonah,
1st Floor, 399 Pitt Street,
Sydney, NSW 2000,
Australia

Rare Animal Relief Effort,
c/- Audubon Society,
950 Third Avenue,
New York, New York 10022,
USA

Yukio Tanaka,
c/- Takano Aparto,
2-7-5 Koraku,
Bunkyo-ku,
Tokyo 112,
Japan

Tasmanian Conservation Trust, Inc.,
GPO Box 6846,
Hobart, Tas 7001,
Australia

Tasmanian Environment Centre,
102 Bathurst Street,
Hobart, Tas 7000,
Australia

Tasmanian Wilderness Society,
28 Criterion Street,
Hobart, Tas 7000,
Australia

Total Environment Centre,
18 Argyle Street,
Sydney, NSW 2000,
Australia

Threshold,
4431 Greenwich Parkway,
Washington, DC 20007,
USA

Sea Shepherd Conservation Society,
Box 306,
Newtown, NSW 2042,
Australia

Sierra Club,
530 Bush Street,
San Francisco, California 94108,
USA

Sierra International,
228 East 45th Street,
New York, New York 10017,
USA

Sierra Club,
330 Pennsylvania Avenue, SE,
Washington, DC 20003,
USA

Society for Animal Protective
   Legislation,
PO Box 3719,
Washington, DC,
USA

Stichting Natuur en Milieu,
Donkerstraat 17,
3511 KB Utrecht,
Netherlands

Washington Humane Society,
7319 Georgia Avenue, NW,
Washington, DC 20011,
USA

Wilderness Society,
1901 Pennsylvania Avenue, NW,
Washington, DC 20006,
USA

Stuurajoeja World Conservation
  Strategy,
Donkerstraat 17,
35 11 KB Utrecht,
Netherlands

Whale Center,
3929 Piedmont Avenue,
Oakland, California 94611,
USA

World Conservation Strategy,
Portbus 7,
3700 AA Zeist,
Netherlands

World League for Protection of
  Animals,
GPO Box 3719,
Sydney, NSW 2001,
Australia

World Wildlife Fund,
937 Chaussee de Waterloo,
B-5 B1180 Brussels,
Belgium

World Wildlife Fund,
60 St Clair Avenue E.,
Suite 201,
Toronto, Ontario M4T IN5,
Canada

World Wildlife Fund,
29 Greville Street,
London EC1N 8AX,
England

Not for Mailing
World Wildlife Fund,
1601 Connecticut Avenue, NW,
Washington, DC 20009,
USA

W. de Savornin Lohnan,
Vereniging Milieudefensie,
2e Wateringplantsoen 9,
Amsterdam,
Netherlands

1. 1979 Letter to President Carter

The President
The White House
Washington, D.C.   16 April 1979

Dear President Carter:

The undersigned environmental and conservation organizations wish to express their serious concern with the emerging United States position regarding future mineral exploitation in Antarctica.

The State Department currently is preparing the U.S. position for the Tenth Consultative Meeting of the Antarctic Treaty Parties in September. A focus of that meeting will be regulation of oil and gas development in Antarctica. The environmental community is greatly concerned that irreversible steps toward oil exploitation may be taken at the Tenth Consultative Meeting without a fair and thorough consideration of the implications and effects of such steps, and without serious thought being given to other alternatives.

We believe that a World Preserve for the Antarctic continent, prohibiting all mineral exploitation until such time as the resources can be obtained without danger to the Antarctic terrestrial and marine ecosystems, is in the best interests of both the United States and the world on environmental, political, economic, and military grounds. We hope that after you have reviewed the situation you will direct the State Department to consider seriously the desirability of the U.S. making such a proposal at the Tenth Consultative Meeting. In particular we are concerned that early oil exploitation

— will damage irrevocably the fragile terrestrial and extremely rich marine Antarctic ecosystems;
— will threaten the successful harvest of Antarctic living marine resources, which could be critical to feeding a hungry world;
— will cause serious international political discord as a result of forcing confrontation on the sovereignty issue, thus jeopardizing the Antarctic Treaty and negotiations in wider international fora; and
— would involve using the oil and gas as an energy source, rather than for such purposes as pharmaceuticals and feedstocks.

Antarctic ecosystems appear to be so fragile that any exploitation activities would produce adverse effects, many of which would be severe and virtually irreversible. Any construction or other surface modification, even before actual exploitation, would destroy the local vegetation and soils. These unique soils would take hundreds or thousands of years to regenerate, if they regenerate at all. Uncovered land that supports plant and animal life is limited to only 2% of the continent, primarily along the coast, and it is precisely those areas that would be prime sites for exploitation and related activities. As you noted in your environmental message of May 23, 1977, "Because this remote, unpopulated region greatly influences the stability of the entire earth's oceans and atmosphere, its unique environment must be preserved."

Development of petroleum resources on the Antarctic continental shelf is of particular concern to us. The harsh weather conditions of the Southern Ocean, particularly the difficulties of dealing with icebergs and pack ice, make the potential for serious spills unacceptably high. Even in more moderate climates it has been impossible to eliminate spills caused by human error, equipment failure, and severe weather conditions. Biodegradation of spilled oil will proceed at a much slower rate than in more temperate waters, subjecting marine life and birds to continued damage from surface coating and ingestion of hydrocarbons. In these circumstances both spills and routine discharges could have catastrophic impacts on living resources, including the endangered great whales, which you have committed yourself to protect, and krill, which form the basis for the entire marine ecosystem. Any adverse effect on krill inevitably will affect virtually all other species in the area.

Far from being of purely environmental concern, these types of impacts would damage the potential for harvesting the food resources of the Southern Ocean. Many experts believe that Antarctic resources can play an important — and perhaps critical — role in providing protein to a hungry world in the future. There have been estimates that the Antarctic fishery could, on a sustainable basis, yield an annual catch as great as that harvested from all the rest of the world's ocean fisheries. As you are aware, the new Antarctic Marine Living Resources Regime is now nearing completion. Questions of sovereignty over fish resources in the 200-mile zones off the continent have created a very difficult negotiating situation, and many important questions, such as catch allocations, have been left for the new Living Resources Commission to resolve. Raising the question of mineral exploitation, which involves much more intense issues of sovereignty, could jeopardize the success of that Regime, to the detriment of the entire world community. It seems very short-sighted to endanger those substantial food resources, either environmentally or politically, without the most pressing need and without the greatest assurances against risk of harm to the environment.

Another environmental consideration is Antarctica's unique capability, as a remote and relatively untouched area, to serve as a monitor for global pollution levels. And, if there is no exploitation of minerals, Antarctica will continue to be a free scientific zone, comprising various unique biological laboratories. In this regard, perpetuation of the Antarctic Treaty, which is based on open scientific research in an atmosphere of cooperation, is critical.

The potential political hazards of pressing forward with an exploitation regime are as great as those for the environment. The U.S. has never filed a territorial claim in Antarctica. Those countries claiming sovereignty over areas of the Antarctic continent will oppose strenuously any attempt to eliminate or override their claims that would allow early U.S. exploitation of minerals. Third World countries, not party to the Antarctic Treaty, consider Antarctica part of the common heritage of mankind. They will likely be fiercely resentful of an attempt by developed states to deprive them of what they consider their fair share of the continent's resources. In contrast, both the Antarctic Treaty parties and other nations would share a common interest in maintaining Antarctica as a preserve for science and food production, with exploitation of resources left to a time in the future when they can be obtained safely and used wisely.

At the Eighth Consultative Meeting in 1975, the U.S. resisted a moratorium on minerals development, favoring instead development of a program that would allow exploration and exploitation when the oil companies are ready. At least one U.S. oil company already has sought permission to conduct exploration activities for oil. Many other countries perceive this as a threat to their own interests, since the U.S. is one of a few nations with the technology to exploit Antarctic minerals in the next twenty years. The political difficulties inherent in negotiating a minerals regime would put great strain on the original Antarctic Treaty, threatening its survival. The collapse of the Antarctic Treaty would have significant political and defense consequences for the U.S. and the world.

In this international political context, the other Consultative Parties could be very receptive to a U.S. initiative for declaring Antarctica a World Preserve, closed to minerals exploitation. The ban on exploitation might be permanent, or for a significant term of years, allowing consensus termination of the ban thereafter. Any change in status for the Preserve, however, should be contingent upon certain further research and technological development and on a well-defined international agreement on use of the resources. As indicated above, the value of petroleum, the mineral most likely to be exploited, may be highest for its unique uses rather than for energy.

Delaying any Antarctic mineral exploration and exploitation for a substantial period, coupled with a firm plan to preserve the free scientific character and demilitarized status of the continent, would be in the long term interests of the entire world community. No such proposal will come from the U.S., however, without a personal directive from the President. Without your intervention, a U.S. position favoring exploration and exploitation of Antarctic minerals will be established by mid-June, 1979.

Mr. President, when you were running for office in 1976, you stated that "[t]he Carter Administration will take the lead in international cooperation to preserve the oceans for the benefit of future generations". Antarctica presents an opportunity for your Administration to promote harmony and equity among nations in the use of scarce resources and protection of the world environment. We hope, after reviewing the facts, that you will direct the State Department to reevaluate the current U.S. position, giving special attention to the suggestion that our nation propose the concept of a World Preserve at the Tenth Consultative Meeting.

Sincerely yours,

James N. Barnes
Janet L. Kleckner
Center for Law and Social Policy

Russell Train
World Wildlife Fund

Brock Evans
Sierra Club

Christopher Roosevelt
The Oceanic Society

Craig Van Note
Monitor, Inc.

David Brower
Friends of the Earth

Anthony Wayne Smith
National Parks and Conservation
   Association

William Butler
Environmental Defense Fund

Lewis Regenstein
Fund for Animals

James Deane
Wilderness Society

Patricia Forkan
Humane Society of the U.S.

Thomas L. Kimball
National Wildlife Federation

Russell Peterson
National Audubon Society

Thomas B. Stoel, Jr.
Natural Resources Defense Council

John Frizell
Greenpeace Foundation

Toby Cooper
Defenders of Wildlife

Hope Robertson
Environmental Policy Center

Donna Hart
International Fund for Animal
   Welfare

Millie Payne
American Cetacean Society

Milton Kaufman
Monitor, International & Let Live

2. 1980 Letter to President Carter

The President
The White House
Washington, D.C.   10 September 1980

Dear President Carter:

Last year twenty environmental organizations wrote you regarding future minerals exploitation in Antarctica and its surrounding waters. We urged that the U.S. consider seriously the desirability, on both environmental and political grounds, of moving to protect the Antarctic region as the first World Preserve. In spite of repeated suggestions that the State Department and other agencies study the possible benefits of protecting Antarctica rather than exploiting it, no agency has indicated a willingness to conduct such an analysis. Instead the U.S. is continuing to be a leader in the movement to establish a legal regime for the Antarctic region that initially would allow oil exploitation on the shelves off the continent, with other minerals to be dealt with later.

Mr. President, the World Conservation Strategy and Global 2000 Report both underline the serious implications for the world if present patterns of resource utilization continue. One key aspect of this is energy use, both in terms of the kind of energy produced and the quantity. These two documents would seem to lend additional support to our proposal to study the full protection option for Antarctica. Such a move would be a significant, symbolic statement that there are limits beyond which the world will not go in its headlong rush to exploit resources.

Antarctic oil surely would be the world's costliest and most dangerous environmentally. At this time even known reserves off areas like Greenland, which are both much closer and uncomplicated with the political difficulties over sovereignty that plague Antarctica, are not being exploited. Antarctic oil reserves are completely speculative at this point. Even if oil were there, there would be little for each country after division of the resources to satisfy the political demands of all Antarctic Treaty Parties. The mere attempt to negotiate such a regime inside the Antarctic Treaty framework will most likely provoke the less developed countries, many of which feel that a few wealthier

nations do not have the right to carve up an area which is not subject to national jurisdiction. Finally, if oil exploitation does take place, the harsh weather and iceberg conditions make spills almost inevitable. Because oil biodegrades so slowly in cold climates, either spills or routine discharges of oil could have catastrophic effects on marine life. Creatures from the tiny krill, which forms the basis of the entire marine ecosystem, to the great whales, now so seriously endangered, could be jeopardized. Industrialization would ruin Antarctica's unique capability to serve as a global monitor for pollution levels.

The U.S. recently experienced great difficulty in negotiating a Convention for the conservation and use of marine life around Antarctica, a resource that is renewable and not commercially valuable at present. The document that resulted is very limited in terms of establishing a decision-making process that can operate to protect the environment in the context of resource utilization. There is every indication that negotiation of an exploration and exploitation regime for oil, which is not renewable and is valuable, will be even more difficult. Any decision-making framework established in a new Antarctic Minerals Convention probably would be no better than the one for living resources, and could be worse. Moreover, the less developed countries, which ignored the living resources negotiations, will be much more interested in oil. Given these facts, it would seem that sound policy requires the U.S. to study seriously the various benefits associated with not moving ahead in a development mode for Antarctic mineral resources.

The undersigned environmental organizations urge you to direct the State Department to analyze carefully all the benefits that would result from acting to protect Antarctica as a World Preserve or World Heritage, or in some other appropriate way. We hope that after reviewing such an analysis you will direct the U.S. representative to propose the World Preserve concept at the 11th Consultative Meeting of the Antarctic Treaty Parties next June in Argentina.

Sincerely yours,

James N. Barnes
Leonard C. Meeker
Clifton E. Curtis
CENTER FOR LAW AND SOCIAL POLICY

Russell Train
WORLD WILDLIFE FUND

Russell Peterson
NATIONAL AUDUBON SOCIETY

Thomas Kimball
NATIONAL WILDLIFE FEDERATION

Eugene Coan
SIERRA CLUB

James Deane
WILDERNESS SOCIETY

David Brower
FRIENDS OF THE EARTH

William Butler
ENVIRONMENTAL DEFENSE FUND

Thomas B. Stoel, Jr.
NATURAL RESOURCES DEFENSE
   COUNCIL

Christoper Roosevelt
OCEANIC SOCIETY

Christine Stevens
SOCIETY FOR ANIMAL PROTECTIVE
   LEGISLATION

Valerie McOuat
GREENPEACE U.S.A.

Toby Cooper
DEFENDERS OF WILDLIFE

Lewis Regenstein
FUND FOR ANIMALS

Patricia Forkan
HUMANE SOCIETY OF THE US

Milton Kaufmann
MONITOR INTERNATIONAL

Maxine McCloskey
WHALE CENTER

Phoebe Wray
CENTER FOR ACTION ON
   ENDANGERED SPECIES

Millie Payne
AMERICAN CETACEAN SOCIETY

Beula Edmiston
FRIENDS OF WILDLIFE

Daniel Morast
INTERNATIONAL FUND FOR ANIMAL
   WELFARE

John Milton
THRESHOLD, INC.

3. 1980 ASOC Letter to Heads of State

Dear Mr. Prime Minister: 21 April 1980
This letter is sent on behalf of the 83 non-governmental organizations joined together in the Antarctic and Southern Ocean Coalition (ASOC). These organizations represent citizens from all over the world.

We commend you and your government for your commitment to negotiate a Convention for the Conservation of Antarctic Marine Living Resources, using an ecosystem approach that requires the impacts of harvesting on dependent species to be taken into account.

May we respectfully call your attention, however, to a number of improvements in the Convention that we consider to be essential? It is our belief that the draft Convention is not adequate in the following important respects:

1. Because of ambiguities in Article II(3)(a) it may not protect species that are dependent on krill;
2. The Convention will not be acceptable to the widest possible number of states;
3. The use of a consensus voting procedure makes it more likely that the Convention will not function effectively than if it incorporated some form of majority voting;
4. There is no provision for adequate enforcement, especially the creation of an effective international inspection system;
5. It does not ensure the full submission and utilization of scientific and technical data; and
6. It does not establish a comprehensive conservation regime south of the Antarctic convergence so as to exclude lower conservation standards in recognized exclusive economic zones.

From our point of view, the Convention appears oriented more toward harvesting than toward protecting and conserving species. Detailed recommendations for amendments to the draft Convention consistent with the above principles are attached for your consideration.

In addition to these recommendations, we understand that your government soon will be receiving the report of a recent international workshop on management of the Southern Ocean ecosystem. This report contains important scientific recommendations for the ecosystem conservation standard set out in Article II and for sound implementation of the Convention, both in the short- and long-term. Incorporation of these recommendations will enhance the Convention's chances for success. We ask you to give them consideration prior to the Canberra meeting.

We also express our great concern that krill harvesting during the next several years, before the Convention enters into force, should not adversely affect endangered whales. We urge conservation safeguards to minimize any risk to organisms of the Southern Ocean prior to the entry into force of the Convention.

Additionally, we ask that your government support a resolution by the Antarctic Treaty Parties at the forthcoming international conference in Australia declaring the 1980s as an International Decade of Southern Ocean Research. This would be an important step to improve our knowledge of Antarctic ecosystems and would help allow sound implementation of the ecosystem standard contained in Article II. Naturally we hope that your government can make appropriate commitments to fund adequate Antarctic research programs during the 1980s.

Finally, may we also enlist your support for the accreditation of ASOC and other national and international non-governmental organizations as observers at the international conference for the Marine Living Resources Convention to be held in Australia in May? ASOC will be representing many NGOs from all over the world. We recommend that accredited NGOs be permitted to participate in plenary sessions and committee meetings. The precedent for NGO participation as accredited observers at such important intergovernmental meetings is well established.

The following non-governmental organizations in the Antarctic and Southern Ocean Coalition join in sending this letter†

THE AMERICAN CETACEAN SOCIETY
USA
THE AMERICAN LITTORAL SOCIETY
USA
THE AMERICAN SOCIETY FOR THE PREVENTION OF
 CRUELTY TO ANIMALS
USA
AMIGOS DE LA NATURALEZA
Costa Rica
AMIGOS DE LA TERRE
Spain
ANIMAL WELFARE INSTITUTE
USA
AN TAISCE
Ireland
AUSTRALIAN CONSERVATION SOCIETY
Australia
AUSTRALIAN NATIONAL PARKS COUNCIL
Australia

BOND BETER LEEFMILIEU
Belgium
CANADIAN NATURE FEDERATION
Canada
THE CENTER FOR ACTION ON ENDANGERED
  SPECIES
USA
CENTER FOR OCEAN STUDIES
USA
CENTRO CIENTIFICO TROPICAL
Costa Rica
FRIENDS OF THE EARTH
Mexico
FRIENDS OF THE EARTH
New Zealand
FRIENDS OF THE EARTH
Scotland
FRIENDS OF THE EARTH
United Kingdom
FRIENDS OF THE EARTH
West Germany
FRIENDS OF THE SEA OTTER
USA
FRIENDS OF WHALES
USA
FRIENDS OF WILDLIFE
USA
FUND FOR ANIMALS
USA
GEELONG ENVIRONMENT COUNCIL
Australia
GREENPEACE
Australia
GREENPEACE
Canada
GREENPEACE
Denmark
GREENPEACE
France
GREENPEACE
Germany
GREENPEACE
Japan
GREENPEACE
Netherlands
GREENPEACE
New Zealand
GREENPEACE
United Kingdom
GREENPEACE
USA
INSTITUTE FOR DELPHINID RESEARCH
Cayman Islands
INTERNATIONAL COUNCIL FOR BIRD
  PRESERVATION
INTERNATIONAL FUND FOR ANIMAL WELFARE
USA

INTERNATIONAL PRIMATE PROTECTION LEAGUE
USA
LAUNCESTON ENVIRONMENT CENTRE
Australia
LET LIVE
USA
LIGUE BELGE POUR LA PROTECTION DES OISEAUX
Belgium
MONITOR INTERNATIONAL
USA
NATIONAL AUDUBON SOCIETY
USA
NATIONAL COALITION FOR MARINE
  CONSERVATION
USA
NATURA
Luxembourg
NATURAL RESOURCES DEFENSE COUNCIL
USA
OCEAN TRUST FOUNDATION
USA
RARE ANIMAL RELIEF FUND
USA
SIERRA CLUB
USA
SOCIETY FOR ANIMAL PROTECTION LEGISLATION
USA
STICHTING NATRUER E MILIEU
Netherlands
TASMANIAN CONSERVATION TRUST, INC.
Australia
TASMANIAN WILDERNESS SOCIETY
Australia
THRESHOLD, INTERNATIONAL CENTER FOR
  ENVIRONMENTAL RENEWAL
USA
TOTAL ENVIRONMENT CENTRE
Australia
WASHINGTON HUMANE SOCIETY
USA
WHALE CENTER
USA
WILDERNESS SOCIETY
USA
WORLD CONSERVATION STATEGY
Netherlands
WORLD WILDLIFE FUND
Belgium
WORLD WILDLIFE FUND
Canada
WORLD WILDLIFE FUND
United Kingdom
WORLD WILDLIFE FUND
USA
VERENIGING MILIEUDEFENSIE
Netherlands

4. MAC Letter to Prime Minister of Australia

The Right Honourable J. M. Fraser, C.H., M.P.
Prime Minister of Australia,
Parliament House,
CANBERRA ACT 2600   24th March, 1980

Dear Prime Minister,

The undersigned environmental and conservation organisations wish to express their serious concern with the present state of negotiations to conclude a marine living resources regime for Antarctica, with the emerging position regarding future mineral exploitation, and with the attitude Australia appears to be adopting towards these crucial issues.

At the Ninth Consultative Meeting in 1977, the Antarctic Treaty parties unanimously agreed to negotiate a convention for the conservation of Antarctic marine living resources, based on an ecosystem approach and thus not limited to commercially exploitable species. In Recommendation IX-2, the parties stated that the new convention ". . . should provide for the effective conservation of the marine living resources of the Antarctic ecosystem as a whole", and that it should safeguard the principles embodied in Article IV of the Antarctic Treaty regarding the rights of territorial claimants and non-claimants ". . . in application to the marine areas south of 60° South latitude". Unfortunately these two principles have proven to be mutually exclusive. The Parties have expended so much energy in protecting their legal positions that they have been unable to focus attention on how best to protect Antarctica.

Everything now indicates that negotiation of the draft "definitive regime" is finalised sufficiently to proceed to the formal international conference to conclude the Convention. The environmental community is gravely concerned that the Convention, if signed in its present form, will become a "seal of approval" for ruthless over-exploitation of the marine environment, and the catastrophic consequences which may result. Further, it will foster the strong possibility of an unstable situation in the future which could jeopardise the Convention and put additional pressures on the Antarctic Treaty.

The Southern Ocean is the home of large populations of living organisms, including fish, seals, squid, penguins, other birds and whales. As you are aware krill is believed to be the primary food for most of these animals, and indirectly affects the rest. In short, krill forms the basis of the Antarctic marine ecosystem. Harvesting of krill in large quantities, especially given our general lack of information about the size of the population, breeding patterns, longevity and interrelationships with other species, presents the potential for serious harm to that ecosystem, and especially the endangered great whales, which you have committed yourself to protect.

Bearing in mind these facts, the environmental community believes that the Convention in its present form is deficient in a number of crucial areas:—

1. The Convention specifically avoids provisions for setting national catch and effort quotas. No doubt this is a deliberate effort to avoid the sovereignty issue and the question of alleged "rights" of claimant states to preferential treatment in their claimed zones. However, without national quotas the effect will be to create a high seas fishery encompassing common resources, and the likely outcome of this will be over-capitalisation of the fishery so typical of such enterprises. Once over-captitalisation has occurred, then the likelihood of any nation curtailing its fishing operations to come into line with scientifically agreed quotas, is extremely remote indeed.

We fear that Australia, as a claimant state, has given its tacit approval to this approach.

2. Attempts to discuss interim conservation measures have so far been blocked by those nations most closely associated with krill harvesting. Since years may elapse before the Convention enters into force, serious damage may have already been done by that time, and the process become irreversible.

The feeling among conservative nations may be that a weak treaty is better than no treaty at all, and arguably certain countries would profit by the lack of a conservation treaty.

However, the question of interim measures will be debated at the final international conference, and we believe it is imperative for those countries committed to conservation principles to vigorously pursue this matter. Conservation-oriented countries must form a united front to state their position forcefully, and not allow a minority of states with selfish interests to dictate, simply because a treaty of some sort, no matter how weak, is the goal. We believe that Australia, if necessary, should take the lead in this issue and, as host nation to the final conference, is in a unique position to do so.

3. Under the present draft Convention, decisions are to be taken by consensus, and coupled to this, Article VIII(6) contains an objection procedure regarding conservation measures. The net result of this voting procedure, plus the lack of interim conservation measures outlined above, may be to make adoption of soundly-based conservation decisions an impossibility.

Clearly we might expect this type of approach from those countries whose interests are primarily exploitative, but they have been aided and abetted by claimant states intent on maintaining self-interest options — for example a desire not to be bound by conservation measures that might restrict exploitation.

For whatever reason, a U.S. proposal for majority voting has never received support. We fear that Australia has not encouraged this proposal because of perceived national interests, and is thus jeopardising the long-term safety of Antarctica for short-term goals.

Environmental groups therefore urge you to strongly support the concept of majority voting coupled, if necessary, to an objection procedure.

These are but a few of the more serious shortcomings of the present draft Marine Living Resources Convention. In essence, the reasons for these are two-fold; firstly, certain nations are intent on exploitation, irrespective of the consequences. Secondly, the question of sovereignty, which has produced a convention existing basically to protect national juridical and fishing interests.

All nations, via the Convention, theoretically accept the need for protection of the Antarctic ecosystem, Australia included. But their first aim is to ensure that any treaty is acceptable to themselves. We are concerned that this attitude compromises the long-term interests of mankind in the preservation of the Antarctic. As Mr. Peacock explained so accurately at the opening of the Second Special Consultative Meeting in Canberra, "The International community will be looking to us to fulfil the responsibilities we have assumed. If we fail in our responses who can say that it will not feel impelled to seek the answers elsewhere. This is both the opportunity and the challenge".

Turning to the question of future mineral exploitation, the under-signed environmental groups fear that such exploitation could damage irrevocably the fragile terrestrial and marine Antarctic ecosystems. Further, the problems of sovereignty already mentioned will be intensified, thus raising the possibility of political discord and increased strain on the Antarctic Treaty.

Antarctic ecosystems appear to be so fragile that any exploitation activities would produce adverse effects, many of which would be severe and virtually irreversible. Any construction or other surface modification, even before actual exploitation, would destroy the local vegetation and soils. These unique soils would take hundreds or thousands of years to regenerate, if they regenerate at all. Uncovered land that supports plant and animal life is limited to only 2% of the continent, primarily along the coast, and it is precisely those areas that would be prime sites for exploitation and related activities.

Development of petroleum resources on the Antarctic continental shelf is of particular concern to us. The harsh weather conditions of the Southern Ocean, particularly the difficulties of dealing with icebergs and pack ice, make the potential for serious oil spills unacceptably high. We must remember that very recently, under *normal* drilling conditions, we have seen the largest oil spill from any source in history. The Pemex well in the Bay of Campeche. At least oil degrades rapidly in moderate climates. But biodegradation of spilled oil will proceed at a much slower rate in Antarctica, subjecting marine life and birds to continued damage from surface coating and ingestion

of hydrocarbons. In these circumstances both spills and routine discharges could have catastrophic effects on living organisms, including krill. And as we have seen, any adverse effect on krill will inevitably affect virtually all other creatures in the area.

Far from being of purely environmental concern, such impacts could seriously damage any potential krill fishery. Harvested along strict environmental lines, and bearing in mind our long-term responsibilities, krill might play a significant part in feeding a hungry world in the future. It would seem very short-sighted to endanger that potential unless we can guarantee that there will be *no* risk of harm to the environment — now or in the future.

The potential political hazards of the minerals question must also be considered. As we have seen, the sovereignty issue has resulted in the living resources regime losing sight of its original objective of conserving the Antarctic marine ecosystem. Already those negotiations have raised questions about the viability of the Antarctic Treaty. Negotiating a minerals regime, which involves much more intense issues of sovereignty, could jeopardise the success of the Antarctic Treaty, to the detriment of the entire world community.

Yet another consideration is Antarctica's unique capability, as a remote and relatively untouched area, to serve as a monitor for global pollution levels. With no exploitation of oil and minerals, Antarctica will continue to be a free scientific zone, comprising various unique biological laboratories — a demilitarised zone reflecting the long-term interest of the world and its peoples. To quote the President of the United States, "because this remote, unpopulated region greatly influences the stability of the earth's oceans and atmosphere, its unique environment must be preserved".

We support the policy of your Government to support ". . . an effective moratorium on the exploration and exploitation of Antarctic mineral resources pending further study of the environmental implications". (Letter from Michael Mackellar 5/10/79). However, it is clear that, given the areas requiring research as outlined by the Group of Experts, it is highly unlikely that sufficient knowledge can be gained to make rational decisions within a reasonable time frame. The only sure way to protect Antarctica is to forego entirely the prospect of mineral developments.

Australia has an outstanding reputation amongst the international community for its conservation policies. That is a reputation of which we are rightly proud. It would be tragic to squander that tradition because of a desire to protect our claims to an Australian Antarctic Territory, and in fact it need not happen. Antarctica is unique, and unquestionably meets the requirements of Natural Heritage in the Convention for the protection of the World Cultural and Natural Heritage. By nominating the Australian Antarctic Territory for inclusion in the World Heritage List, Australia would create the precedent, and provide the impetus for all Antarctic Treaty nations to join in declaring Antarctica a World Preserve.

By this means the major political difficulties can be overcome, and the great achievements of the Antarctic Treaty can be maintained in the future. The Treaty parties would then be free to negotiate a sound Marine Living Resources Convention, free from the problems of sovereignty which so bedevil the present negotiations, and Third World countries would have no quarrel with preserving Antarctica for science and sensible food production.

No such proposal can come from Australia, however, without your personal directive. Your Administration's attitude towards the whaling question has shown to us that you are prepared to take whatever steps are necessary for conservation when the facts warrant. In the short term we believe that Australia must lead the fight for effective conservation of the Antarctic marine ecosystem via the Marine Living Resources negotiations. To this end the environmental community asks you to consider the inclusion of representatives from among us on the Australian delegation at these negotiations. In the longer term, Antarctica represents an opportunity for your Administration to promote harmony and equity among nations in the use of scarce resources and protection of the world environment. We hope, after re-

viewing the facts, that you will direct the Department of Foreign Affairs to re-evaluate the Australian position on Antarctica, giving special consideration to the inclusion of the Australian Antarctic Territory in the World Heritage List as the first step towards declaring Antarctica a World Preserve.

In conclusion, we would respectfully suggest that the Department of Foreign Affairs and other Government departments involved with Antarctica, concerned environmental organisations and members of the public be allowed to express their views on Australia's Antarctic responsibilities before a full and official public inquiry. An indication of the Australian Government's views on such a proposal would be appreciated.

Furthermore, we would very much like to know, in light of the views expressed in this letter, what stand the Australian Government will take at the forthcoming Antarctic Convention on Marine Living Resources.

Ross Burton,
Michael Kennedy
Marine Action Centre Australia

Brian Appleford
Antarctic Defence Coalition

Dr. J.G. Mosley
Australian Conservation
Foundation

Ann Evers
Barrier Environment Group

Haydn Washington
Colo Committee

Geoff Wescott
Conservation Council of Victoria

John Sibly
Conservation Council of
South Australia Inc.

Dr. K.D. Suter
Friends of the Earth
Australia

John Hoey
Greenpeace Australia

Russell Fisher
Kosciusko Committee

Dr. Richard Mason
National Parks Association
of New South Wales

Len Willan
Nature Conservation
Council of New South Wales

Tony Gregory
Project Jonah Australia

Bob McMillan
Protect the Ecology of
Antarctica and the Southern Ocean

Dr. David Lewis
Oceanic Research Foundation

Ray Hammond
South East Conservation
Association Inc.

Dr. Bob Brown
Tasmanian Wilderness Society

Vincent Serventy
Wildlife Preservation Society
of Australia

Fay Smith
Wide Bay Burnett
Conservation Council

Richard Jones
The Fund for Animals Inc.
(Australia)

Milo Dunphy
Total Environment Centre

Louise Horsfall
Tasmanian Conservation
Trust Inc.

Joy Young
World League for Protection
of Animals (Australia)

Bruce Davis
Australian National Parks
Council

R.T. Baker
Environment Council of
the Northern Territory Inc.

ASOC Contribution Form

ANTARCTIC AND SOUTHERN OCEAN COALITION

P.O. BOX 371, MANLY, 2095, N.S.W., AUSTRALIA. TELE: 02 9771557 TELEX 72577
1751 N STREET N.W., WASHINGTON, D.C. 20036, U.S.A. TELE: 202 872 0670

SUPPORT THE SOUTHERN OCEAN COALITION IN ITS CAMPAIGN TO:

- Protect Antarctica from all mineral and oil exploration and expoloitation by designating Antarctica a World Park or heritage monument

- Protect endangered and threatened whales

- Urge governments to implement the Convention on the Conservation of Antarctic Marine Living Resources with its innovative ecosystem approach.

Funds are needed urgently to promote this campaign. Information on a regular basis will be supplied to all contributors to ASOC.

☐ $10 Retired/Student/Low income

☐ $25 Regular

☐ $50 Supporting

☐ Other/Donation ....

Name ....

Address ....

....

Membership Form for The Antarctica Project

THE ANTARCTICA PROJECT

P.O. BOX 371, MANLY, 2095, N.S.W., AUSTRALIA. TELE: 02 9771557 TELEX 72577
1751 N STREET N.W., WASHINGTON, D.C. 20036, U.S.A. TELE: 202 872 0670

BECOME A FRIEND OF ANTARCTICA. YOUR MEMBERSHIP WILL HELP BUILD A CITIZENS' ORGANIZATION WORLDWIDE.

☐ $12 Retired/Student/Low income

☐ $25 Regular

☐ $50 Supporting

☐ $100 for 5 year member

☐ $500 Life Member

☐ $1,000 Patron

☐ Other/Donation ....

Name ....

Address ....

....

ANTARCTIC AND SOUTHERN OCEAN COALITION

PETITION

ANTARCTICA

WE THE UNDERSIGNED CALL UPON THE ANTARCTIC TREATY POWERS AND THE UNITED NATIONS
GENERAL ASSEMBLY TO TAKE IMMEDIATE STEPS TO DECLARE ANTARCTICA A WORLD PARK, IN
RECOGNITION OF ITS INESTIMABLE VALUE TO HUMANKIND, AND ITS STATUS AS A GLOBAL
COMMONS. WE WANT TO SAVE ANTARCTICA FROM ENVIRONMENTAL DESTRUCTION, AND TO ENSURE
THAT THE GREAT WHALES, SEALS, BIRDS AND ALL OTHER FORMS OF WILDLIFE ARE PRESERVED
FOR THE BENEFIT OF FUTURE GENERATIONS.

Name	Address	Signature

Name	Address	Signature

PLEASE RETURN TO: ANTARCTIC AND SOUTHERN OCEAN COALITION

ANTARCTIC AND SOUTHERN OCEAN COALITION

PETITION

ANTARCTICA

WE THE UNDERSIGNED CALL UPON THE ANTARCTIC TREATY POWERS AND THE UNITED NATIONS GENERAL ASSEMBLY TO TAKE IMMEDIATE STEPS TO DECLARE ANTARCTICA A WORLD PARK, IN RECOGNITION OF ITS INESTIMABLE VALUE TO HUMANKIND, AND ITS STATUS AS A GLOBAL COMMONS. WE WANT TO SAVE ANTARCTICA FROM ENVIRONMENTAL DESTRUCTION, AND TO ENSURE THAT THE GREAT WHALES, SEALS, BIRDS AND ALL OTHER FORMS OF WILDLIFE ARE PRESERVED FOR THE BENEFIT OF FUTURE GENERATIONS.

Name	Address	Signature

Name	Address	Signature

PLEASE RETURN TO: ANTARCTIC AND SOUTHERN OCEAN COALITION